POETS OF NORTH CAROLINA

POETS
OF
NORTH CAROLINA

Edited by

RICHARD WALSER

The University of North Carolina Press
Chapel Hill

COPYRIGHT © 1963 BY
RICHARD WALSER

Library of Congress Catalog Card Number 63-14628
MANUFACTURED IN THE UNITED STATES OF AMERICA

ACKNOWLEDGMENTS

ALL RIGHTS to the poems in this collection remain under the control of those publishers and authors (and in one case an executor) given below. For permission to reprint in this book certain copyrighted material as well as poems printed for the first time, grateful appreciation is hereby extended.

JAMES LARKIN PEARSON. All poems from *Selected Poems of James Larkin Pearson.* By permission of the author and the publisher, McNally of Charlotte.

OLIVE TILFORD DARGAN. All poems from *The Spotted Hawk,* copyright 1958 by John F. Blair, publisher. By permission of publisher.

PAUL BARTLETT. "Apology," "Finale," and "Lèse Majesté" from *Moods and Memories* (Heritage House, Charlotte) and "City Rain," "Love's Ending," and "So Independently the Cedars Grow" from *And What of Spring?* (Traversity Press, Penobscot, Maine). By permission of author.

EDITH EARNSHAW. Except for "They Roasted Me Instead," "He Will Make the Grade," "Two Little Houses," "Miss Flo," and "Query," all poems from *Verses.* By permission of Worth Copeland, executor of the Estate of Mrs. Edith T. Earnshaw.

ZOE KINCAID BROCKMAN. "A Cold Wind Blows," "The Dream Is Not Enough," "Christmas Eve," "To the Lost Colony," and "Three Cinquains" from *Heart on My Sleeve.* All poems by permission of author.

HELEN BEVINGTON. "A Bowl of October," "Find Out Moonshine," "Report from the Carolinas," "Summer Excursion: Signs and Portents," and "The Magnolia Belt" from *A Change of Sky,* published by Houghton Mifflin Company. "The New Letter Writer," "A Street in North Carolina," "A Way of Looking," and "September Winds" from *When Found, Make a Verse Of,* copyright 1961, published by Simon and Schuster, Inc. By permission of author and publishers.

JAMES SEXTON LAYTON. All three poems from *The Enchanted Garden,* published by Vantage Press. By permission of author.

VERNON WARD. Except for "Mixed Emotions" and "Heart Path," selections from *Of Dust and Stars,* published by Exposition Press. All poems by permission of author.

RANDALL JARRELL. "A Sick Child" and "A Girl in a Library" from *The Seven-League Crutches*, copyright 1951 by Randall Jarrell. Reprinted by permission of Harcourt, Brace & World, Inc.

SAM RAGAN. All poems by permission of author.

THAD STEM, JR. "Crisis," "Sure Sign," "Church Bell—Winter Time," "School Days," "Courthouse Bell," and "Boy on the Back of a Wagon" from *The Jackknife Horse* (Wolfe's Head Press). "Man Raking Leaves," "Blotting Paper," "Post Card," "Old Hup," "Deep Summer, after Midnight," "Little Saucers, Big Saucers," and "Something More" from *Penny Whistles and Wild Plums*, published by McNally and Loftin. All poems by permission of publishers and author.

CHARLES EDWARD EATON. "Carol," "The Waves," "Copperhead," "A Love-Death Story," and "Crepe Myrtle" from *The Greenhouse in the Garden*, by permission of Twayne Publishers, Inc. "The Compleat Swimmer," "In the Headlights," and "Notes for an Autobiography" from *Countermoves*, copyright 1962 by Charles Edward Eaton, published by Abelard-Schuman. By permission of publisher and author.

FRANK BORDEN HANES. "In Labyrinths" and "The Plain Man" (untitled in the original) reprinted from *Abel Anders* by Frank Borden Hanes, by permission of Farrar, Straus & Cudahy, Copyright © 1951 by Frank Borden Hanes. Other poems by permission of author.

ELEANOR ROSS TAYLOR. All poems from *Wilderness of Ladies*, Copyright, 1960, Eleanor Ross Taylor author, reprinted with the permission of Ivan Obolensky, Inc., New York.

WILL INMAN. "Where Willow Is a Limber Switch," "Tree Will Mow Thickets," and "Dilation" from *Lament and Psalm;* "On Seven Hills," "The Distance in Your Touch," "Lyric," and "A Blown Newspaper" from *A River of Laughter;* "Be" from *Honey in Hot Blood*. By permission of author.

GUY OWEN. All poems, with revisions, from *Cape Fear Country*, except for "Deserted Farm" and "Split-Rail Fence." By permission of author.

ROBERT WATSON. All poems by permission of author, who retains full rights.

O. B. HARDISON, JR. All poems by permission of author. "Impressions" from *Southern Poetry Today*, edited by Guy Owen and William E. Taylor. "Of Motion" from *Epos*.

JONATHAN WILLIAMS. "Our Dusk: That West" from *Four Stoppages* (Jargon); "Credo" and "Fast Ball" from *The Empire Finals at Verona* (Jargon); "3 Sit-Ins Agin . . ." from *Carolina Quarterly*, Summer, 1960; "The Rough Day" and "A Spin" from *Amen/Huzza/Selah* (Jargon); "Cobwebbery" and "The Flower-Hunter in the Fields" from *In England's Green &* (The Auerhahn Press, San Francisco). By permission of author.

H. A. SIEBER. "Oakdale Angel," "October," "Blue Ridge Parkway," and "On the Make-Up of a Poet" from *In This the Marian Year*. "The Saint and the Poet," "Something the West Will Remember," and "From the Alembic" from *Something the West Will Remember*. All poems by permission of author.

PREFACE

WHEN AN EDITOR issues a collection of works by twenty contemporary poets, the reader is due an explanation. This is true even when the collection is limited to one region, one state. There comes the question: Can North Carolina be very different—in literature, in poetry—from other states? The answer, of course, is yes. North Carolina is different because the climate is different, the geography is different, the racial heritage is different, the history has been different, the directions of education and politics and thought have been different, and particularly because the individual writers in the state have been different from those elsewhere.

It is not that North Carolina is an isolated region, cut off culturally from the rest of the literary world. Literary trends and fashions, whether they originate in North Carolina or New York or in France or Japan, influence writing no matter where the author was born or now lives. He is an adjunct of his era, and his words convey his observations and ruminations. Even so, here in North Carolina the poet is different in his environment and, more notably of course, in the distinction of his individual personality. The North Carolina poet is separated from his fellows because of his connection with the people of a state which is not quite like any other geographical area.

To read the lines of the composite North Carolina poet in this book is, I believe, to come upon the composite conscience of a state. "The poet is the intense center of the life of his age," says one of James Joyce's characters. More than the physician, the newspaperman, the preacher, the teacher—the poet frees himself of all except that which is truth to him. Even at those times when he cannot attain unrestricted truth, he is an *intense center* about which life revolves and which he records. Our best poets acquaint us with our keenest sensibilities.

It seems to me that such an opportunity for wisdom, even on a regional basis, is sufficient apologia for this collection of poems by North Carolinians.

No one will contest the statement that we live in a perplexed age: an age in which man is confused. If the poet occupies the *center*, he naturally reflects this turmoil, frequently twisting from abject despair to a beatific optimism. Often these wrestings are apparent not only in the subject matter of his poem, but also in its design and technique.

Recently an art friend and I were talking about a contemporary painting to which I had reacted with an indifference just short of annoyance. He said that he had liked the abstract canvas very much and, knowing my usual receptivity to modern art, expressed surprise at my attitude. "How long did you look at it?" he asked. I saw at once the drift of his attack, and admitted honestly that I had given it hardly more than a glance. "Well," he came back at me, "if you gave it less than five minutes, you can't really be sure that you didn't like it." Of course, he was right and later I went back to the gallery, spent fifteen (not five) minutes before the painting, and came away with a humble, genuine respect for the artist.

The poet is like the painter. He cannot always be counted on to reveal his subtleties at a moment's contact. As the art of painting is not mere decoration, neither is poetry mere everyday prose. If a poet appeals to us with immediacy, well and good. Yet it is likely that, if he is worth his salt, a renewed familiarity with his lines will bring new understandings. On the other hand, if he does not appeal to us at first reading, is it not possible that, like the artist, he is asking for a second, a third, perhaps even a tenth exposure?

The complexion and disposition of contemporary times are not so clearly defined as those of past centuries, when even a famed poem like Shelley's "Adonais" strained many an intellect. There is all the more need, then, for multiple exposure to the poets of our own day who, though not always enigmatic, are neither always so lucid as we might wish them to be.

To enjoy poetry (and enjoyment, even more than wisdom, is a desideratum in poetry), the reader must first accept the premise that the poet is the conscience of his time. He is therefore worth our effort and our attention. In North Carolina the poet has functioned as commentator and interpreter since the eighteenth century, and the state has not lacked those like myself to bring into one book the collective poetic voice of its age.

In 1854, Mary Bayard Clarke issued *Wood-Notes; or, Carolina Carols: A Collection of North Carolina Poetry* in a handsome two-volume edition. In her Preface, Mrs. Clarke wrote: "As the note of the mocking-bird in our native woods is sweeter to the ear of patriotism than the song of the nightingale in foreign climes, so it is hoped that these Wood-Notes will be dear to North Carolinians." William Gaston, Robert Strange, and a few others among the sixty authors are recalled today as political figures, not poets. The pages contain little worth preserving except the lines by Mrs. Clarke herself ("Tenella"), "The Lion and the Terrapin" by America's first novelist William Hill Brown, and the annonymous "Swannanoa." Presumably Mrs. Clarke was unaware of the poems written about 1760 by Thomas Godfrey in Wilmington, or those by Governor Thomas Burke of Revolutionary times, or of the two books by George Moses Horton, the remarkable slave-poet of Chapel Hill.

In 1894 Hight C. Moore brought out *Select Poetry of North Carolina*, stating that he hoped it would "prove a stimulus to native literature." Instead of duplicating the selections in *Wood-Notes*, Moore covered the intervening forty years. Among his forty-one poets, some names now remembered faintly are John Henry Boner, Edwin Wiley Fuller, Theophilus Hunter Hill, Christian Reid, and Henry Jerome Stockard.

By 1912, when E. C. Brooks published *North Carolina Poems* for use in the schools, Benjamin Sledd and John Charles McNeill had achieved some distinction and were adequately represented. Brooks included a few early poets but affirmed that the best of his contributors had "lived and wrought almost within this generation."

In 1941, when I edited a first edition of *North Carolina Poetry*, I reached back to Thomas Godfrey, gathered prominent names from the nineteenth century, and brought the survey up to date with contemporary writers like Struthers Burt, Rebecca Cushman, Anne Blackwell Payne, Andrew Hewitt, and Stewart Atkins. I also included some of the poetic prose by Paul Green and Thomas Wolfe. In 1951, in a second edition of *North Carolina Poetry*, I eliminated a few names and added seven poets who had come to the fore during the decade.

Some time ago, when this second edition went out of print, a normal impulse was to make revisions for a third book in a similar fashion. Instead, however, the publisher and I decided to issue a volume which would be almost entirely new, to change the title somewhat to signify this, and to confine the selections to those by poets who were living and had been rather actively engaged in writing poems for the past dozen years. Though Edith Earnshaw died after the policy was charted, we concluded to go through with the original list.

Since World War II, poetry in North Carolina has undergone a particularly creative period. To the one who reads the work of poets, this statement is all too obvious. There has been an excitement of new subjects, new forms, new techniques. By limiting the number of the poets represented in this volume to twenty, I trust I have been able, without undue repetition, to illustrate these new poetic extensions and to give a rather full number of pages to each poet.

Since this book is rather broadly titled *Poets of North Carolina,* the reader expecting examples of poetry dating from the middle of the eighteenth century on may perhaps be disappointed. The primary regret will be the omission of John Charles McNeill, who died in 1907. But the two little volumes by McNeill are still in print and may easily be obtained. Currently in print, too, are collections by Governor Burke, John Henry Boner, and other names from the past.

In a different connection, I find it curious to note that only three authors from my 1941 edition are still present in 1963: James Larkin Pearson, Olive Tilford Dargan, and Zoe Kincaid Brockman. Hold-overs from 1951 are those three, in addition to Helen Bevington, Randall Jarrell, Thad Stem, Jr., and Charles Edward Eaton. The other thirteen writers in the present book are included in an anthology of North Carolina poetry for the first time. No poems from the other two editions reappear except for a few long-admired stanzas by Pearson and Mrs. Brockman. Sadly I report that copyright restrictions prevented my including any of the work of Carl Sandburg. Also, copyright limitations qualified the selections of three other writers, who in spite of this handicap have nevertheless been presented with excellent exemplary poems.

The growing interest in the writing of poetry in North Carolina today has been due to a number of factors, one of them certainly not that the poet's reading public has expanded.

The audience for even the most acclaimed poet is still very small, and except in rare cases his books go unsold and unread. But other influences have kept him busy, even when he felt he was not getting the readership he wished to have and felt he deserved.

The North Carolina Poetry Society and the Poetry Council of North Carolina, both statewide organizations, woo writers with numerous awards and cash prizes. Many county and regional cultural groups recognize poets at yearly festivals. As a result, winners are likely to get their names and pictures in the newspapers, even when their poems remain unprinted.

In 1953 the Roanoke-Chowan Poetry Cup was established and its administration put into the hands of the North Carolina Literary and Historical Association. Over a ten-year period, seven poets have won the cup for published books either once or twice: Frank Borden Hanes, Thad Stem, Jr., Helen Bevington, Dorothy Edwards Summerow, Paul Bartlett, Olive Tilford Dargan, and Carl Sandburg.

This public recognition of the poet has not, however, been matched by any encouragement of publication. One newspaper in the state, the Raleigh *News and Observer,* uses an original poem on its editorial page every day of the year; and several writers have developed under the aegis of this receptivity. Other newspapers seem to avoid poetry as if it were in some way simply unnecessary for daily consumption. Though a few campus periodicals, like the *Carolina Quarterly* at Chapel Hill, print poems, none of the more widely distributed state journals do.

Nowadays the publication of a book presents obstacles so staggering that the average manuscript never meets a typesetter. If the author is relatively unknown or if his endorsement has been merely local, no publisher will feel that a risk can be taken on a book—no matter how good the poetry. In that case, the poet must either abandon his plans, or himself finance his opus. Even then, only in unusual cases will the publication repay the author's expenses.

The picture is certainly not disheartening for the assiduous professional poet who has built his literary career on first placing his work in national journals before contemplating a book. With a bank of dignified periodical listings behind him, he will probably have, and usually does, an excellent chance with a New York publisher or an established provincial one. Most of the poets in this book have in general followed this procedure.

Whatever the heart-breaks or successes, the poet is a hardy spirit, seldom influenced by fortune of any sort to forsake the thing he loves. And this is a good thing for all of us—for among us the poet is one of those few who are at the *center* and who dare speak out with beauty and fearlessness and honesty.

Of the twenty poets in this collection, it is my belief that each one has a way and a style so individual that anyone thoroughly familiar with his work would not fail to identify the author of his lines, even though the poem was new to him and no name was attached. It is also my belief that each of the twenty has some unusual technique to display, some worthwhile observations to make, and some truth to expound.

Now for some statistics: Only two of the twenty poets, Eleanor Ross Taylor and Will Inman, live outside the state, though Charles Edward Eaton spends part of the year away. Fifteen were born in North Carolina. The five who are not natives—Olive Tilford Dargan, Paul Bartlett, Helen Bevington, Randall Jarrell, and Robert Watson—have now been in North Carolina for a decade or longer, have homes here, and apparently are permanent residents.

A number of the poets are lucky enough to be "at liberty" —at least as far as pay-check occupations go. Of the others, Paul Bartlett is an artist, Thad Stem, Jr., is a government employee, Will Inman is a librarian, Jonathan Williams is in publishing, and H. A. Sieber works for a health organization. Zoe Kincaid Brockman and Sam Ragan are journalists. Not at all surprising is that six of the twenty are college teachers of English: Helen Bevington, Vernon Ward, Randall Jarrell, Guy Owen, Robert Watson, and O. B. Hardison, Jr. In these days when the writing of poetry is almost never remunerative, colleges and universities have gladly opened their academic doors to poets who are also willing to teach. There is, needless to say, a certain prestige in having an established, practicing poet on the staff of a Department of English whose main purpose is the study of language and literature. It is curious to note that, of the twenty, only five—Olive Tilford Dargan, Zoe Kincaid Brockman, James Sexton Layton, Thad Stem, Jr., and Jonathan

Williams—have not settled in what might be called a college community.

When I earlier mentioned "the composite conscience of a state," by no means did I intend to imply that all twenty poets produce a sort of unanimity. A composite is diverse. And so are the intentions and perspectives and styles of these twenty poets, and often within their own work. Yet, even though labels can be misleading and are frequently inaccurate, a grouping to indicate some of the aspects of this diversity may be helpful to the reader.

Reasonably orthodox are the techniques of poets such as James Larkin Pearson, Olive Tilford Dargan, Paul Bartlett, Zoe Kincaid Brockman, and James Sexton Layton. Meter, rhyme, and stanza form (the sonnet, for instance) are more noticeable than absent. The conventions are observed, even in Pearson's dialect verse.

A second group who may be called by the general word formalistic is composed of Randall Jarrell, Charles Edward Eaton, Frank Borden Hanes, Eleanor Ross Taylor, Guy Owen, Robert Watson, and O. B. Hardison, Jr. These poets have not forsaken the traditions; rather they have extended them, particularly in the structure of the poem itself, to serve the need and purpose of the moment. Almost always there is a visible pattern. This rule of thumb is somewhat less true in the work of Sam Ragan and Thad Stem, Jr.

Those who seem consciously to be breaking forms are Vernon Ward, Will Inman, Jonathan Williams, and H. A. Sieber, and thus they may be termed antiformalistic. Their experiments are easily recognizable.

Wit and humor are abundant throughout the book, as in the poems, otherwise so different, by James Larkin Pearson, Robert Watson, O. B. Hardison, Jr., and Jonathan Williams. Two poets, though, have become particularly identified as humorists: Edith Earnshaw with her folksy rhythms, and Helen Bevington with poems quite sophisticated indeed.

As for subject matter, a regional anthologist is always tempted to choose an ample selection of those which bear directly on the geographical area. That I have not completely resisted the temptation is attested by the inclusion of poems like Sam Ragan's "Gray Horizons" about our seacoast, poems like Charles Edward Eaton's "Crepe Myrtle" and Helen Bevington's "The Magnolia Belt," poems like H. A. Sieber's

"Blue Ridge Parkway." But, then, they are all good poems; and why not have them, whether they have been inspired by the North Carolina scene or not? Yet, this aspect of editing aside, I have been motivated in selection, I prayfully trust, primarily by what I thought to be the worth and attractiveness of the individual poems.

Introducing each poet's section are additional comments, both biographical and critical. The poems themselves, from the most traditional to the most unconventional, are, I believe, representative of the best poetry being written in North Carolina.

R. W.

Department of English
North Carolina State College
Raleigh, 23 February 1963

CONTENTS

Acknowledgments	v
Preface	ix
JAMES LARKIN PEARSON	1
OLIVE TILFORD DARGAN	9
PAUL BARTLETT	22
EDITH EARNSHAW	26
ZOE KINCAID BROCKMAN	35
HELEN BEVINGTON	41
JAMES SEXTON LAYTON	48
VERNON WARD	52
RANDALL JARRELL	59
SAM RAGAN	64
THAD STEM, JR.	70
CHARLES EDWARD EATON	79
FRANK BORDEN HANES	86
ELEANOR ROSS TAYLOR	92
WILL INMAN	100
GUY OWEN	106
ROBERT WATSON	112
O. B. HARDISON, JR.	117
JONATHAN WILLIAMS	123
H. A. SIEBER	131
Index to Poems	139

JAMES LARKIN PEARSON

ON AUGUST 4, 1953, Governor William B. Umstead appointed James Larkin Pearson the official Poet Laureate of North Carolina. It was the climax of a writer's career devoted to poetry. When the position became vacant, recommendations from all over the state had been unanimously in favor of Pearson, who had long been unofficially called the poet laureate of his region.

Pearson was born on a hilltop in Wilkes County (see his poem "Fifty Acres"), September 13, 1879. On a chilly winter's day, at the age of four, he spoke his first rhyme:
>My fingers and my toes,
>My feet and my hands,
>Are just as cold as
>You ever see'd a man's.

Little verses kept popping into his head as he worked on the mountain farm and attended the short-term rural schools. At sixteen, his first poem was published. When he was twenty-one, he learned the printer's trade and soon was involved in politics. After his first marriage, he edited a successful monthly newspaper *The Fool Killer* for nearly twenty years, and there he printed numerous occasional poems. During the 1930's, following the death of his wife, he spent five lonely years at Fifty Acres, then in 1939 moved to Guilford College, the home of his second wife, the writer Eleanor Louise Fox, who died in 1962. Since then, he has lived intermittently with his foster daughter, Mrs. Albert Eller of North Wilkesboro.

Five books of poetry—*Castle Gates* (1908), *Pearson's Poems* (1924), *Fifty Acres* (1937), *Plowed Ground* (1949), and *Early Harvest* (1952)—were printed by the poet on his own press, and consequently are collector's items. The publication of *The Selected Poems of James Larkin Pearson* (1960), sponsored by the Poetry Council of North Carolina, drew on established favorites, but also added new material. Pearson's work, whether lyrics or dialect verse, is defined by the solid values and forms which he learned as a young man. Always his aim has been to improve his technique and to reassert his belief in the worth of integrity and delight and love.

FIFTY ACRES

I've never been to London,
　　I've never been to Rome;
But on my Fifty Acres
　　I travel here at home.

The hill that looks upon me
　　Right here where I was born
Shall be my mighty Jungfrau,
　　My Alp, my Matterhorn.

A little land of Egypt
　　My meadow plot shall be,
With pyramids of hay-stacks
　　Along its sheltered lee.

My hundred yards of brooklet
　　Shall fancy's faith beguile,
And be my Rhine, my Avon,
　　My Amazon, my Nile.

My humble bed of roses,
　　My honeysuckle hedge,
Will do for all the gardens
　　At all the far world's edge.

In June I find the Tropics
　　Camped all about the place;
Then white December shows me
　　The Arctic's frozen face.

My wood-lot grows an Arden,
　　My pond a Caspian Sea;
And so my Fifty Acres
　　Is all the world to me.

Here on my Fifty Acres
　　I safe at home remain,
And have my own Bermuda,
　　My Sicily, my Spain.

HOMER IN A GARDEN

A sheltered garden in a sheltered land,
   A pleasant seat upon the mossy ground,
A book of Homer open in my hand,
   And languorous sweet odors all around.

Then suddenly the ages fell away,
   My sheltered garden floated off in space,
And on some lost millennium's bloody day
   I stood with storied Ilium face to face.

The honeysuckle smells that would not fade
   Hung like a ghost above the field of red,
And every dreaming pansy-face was made
   The likeness of the faces of the dead.

Such wonders were abroad in all the land,
   Such magic did the mighty gods employ,
That every lily was a Helen's hand
   And every rose a burning tower of Troy.

GOD

When young Eternity was born
   In days that never can be told—
In some far-off forgotten morn—
   Then God was old.

When old Eternity lies dead
   The awful wreck of worlds among,
And every sun and star has fled,
   God will be young.

ROOMMATES

My feet live here in a small house;
   My heart goes out and in;
And my stay-at-home feet never know
   Where my travelling heart has been.

HERE IS WISDOM

Old Andy never went to school
    And never read a book;
But he who takes him for a fool
    Will need a second look.
He knows more things than anyone
    That you'll be apt to meet,
And on all questions 'neath the sun
    His knowledge is complete.

Old Bobsy went to school a bit,
    And he has read a heap,
And often keeps his candles lit
    While Andy lies asleep.
But Bobsy isn't quite so sure
    Of quite so many things,
For questions rise and doubts allure
    And faith has broken wings.

Old Jasper sports an LL.D.
    And Ph.D. as well
And every other high degree
    The colleges will sell.
But Jasper only shakes his head
    At questions great and small
And seems to know, when truth is said,
    Not anything at all.

A NIGHT IN JUNE

The June-bug roosted under a leaf,
    And the fire-fly winked at the cricket;
The bull-frog sang from the lily-pond
    To the owl in the ivy thicket.

The old mule switched his bushy tail,
    Now free from the tiresome crupper;
The toad licked out his long red tongue
    And caught him a fly for supper.

The whippoorwills met in the twilight air
   And there held a conference, maybe;
The old cow stood by the pasture gate
   And lowed to her bovine baby.

The house-dog howled at the rising moon
   By simply the force of habit;
The fox crawled through the old brush fence
   And raised his hat to the rabbit.

I AIN'T NO CANDIDATE

I couldn't hold no office job
   Ner run no government;
I couldn't face the frownin' mob
   Ner quell the discontent.

I couldn't mount no cracker-box
   An' wave my arms an' yell,
An' say the country's on the rocks
   An' goin' plum to hell.

I ain't no hand at slappin' backs
   Ner tellin' campaign jokes
Ner puttin' on no phony acts
   To fool the common folks.

I ain't got no ambitious plans
   To be somebody great
With lots of business on my hands
   An' big affairs of state.

This singin' job is better fun—
   It's what I understand;
An' when thar's *restin'* to be done,
   I make a reg'lar hand.

EROSION

When I have rested dead a thousand years
   Till frost and rain have weathered down the hill,
Till my dead dust as surface sand appears
   And down eroded ruts my ashes spill,
The brook will take me to its singing heart
   And bear me on triumphant to the sea
Till every land shall claim a little part
   And naught can be identified as me.

Will I be gone? Or will my dust return
   From all the washing of the seven seas
To find my lost identity and learn
   To make new verses as I now make these?
If Gabriel wakes a poet when he blows,
I'll all be back together, I suppose.

WILD GARDEN

So prim and proper in its guarded close,
   With all its hedges trimmed exactly right,
With perfect plants all set in perfect rows
   And not a weed nor rebel thing in sight:
   It well may be the gardener's delight
     To tend and keep it subject to his will,
   Demanding, as it does, an endless fight
     With wild and evil things that he must kill.

But never did a garden love its keeper
   Nor give itself quite freely to his hand.
Its heart is wild, its jungle sense is deeper
   Than its fine manners all so bravely planned.
Turn any garden loose: it will depart
And seek its level in the jungle's heart.

OCTOBER DAYS

These are the days that come on silent feet
   Like mourners in a house where lie the dead,
When autumn's gathered glory is complete
   And all the fevered world of brown and red
Is waiting for its beauty to be shed
   In lavish waste upon the frosted ground—
A captive princess unto prison led,
   A bride unhusbanded, a queen uncrowned.

These are the days of silence and sad smiles,
   The mellow, memoried evening of the year,
When garnered harvest in abundant piles
   Can scarce restrain the slow, unbidden tear.
Half-dreaming world, too rare for poet's praise,
So sweet—so sad—the dear October days!

BIRTHPLACE

When I would boast of my log-cabin birth
   And claim with Lincoln and with Burns a share
   Of all the hard-bought honors that they bear
From splendid battles with the savage earth,
Lo, sudden check is put upon my mirth,
   And in strange silence I become aware
   Of one great Presence, dazzling and most fair—
One humbly born, yet of eternal worth.

More glory than a cabin may bestow,
   Or meanest hut bequeath to favored son,
     Is linked forever with an ox's stall;
For in the ox's manger, lying low,
   The seeking shepherds found the Perfect One
     Who claims our adoration more than all.

ONE-TALENT MAN

God gave one little talent to his keeping—
    A barren thing—the doubtful gift of song.
Day after day, heart-sick and spent with weeping,
    He cried his wares to all the heedless throng.
They tossed him fame, as oft a careless penny
    Is flung to any beggar in the street.
(The beggars are so hungry and so many,
    And who should worry if they do not eat?)

They found him starving on a mouldy crust
    (So small a harvest for so great a reaping).
They gave him back to silence and to dust,
    And on the slab whereunder he lies sleeping
They carved a line to hold his fame in trust:
    "God gave one little talent to his keeping."

OLIVE TILFORD DARGAN

Though Olive Tilford Dargan is a novelist and short story writer of note, her first published work, *Semiramis* (1906), was a closet drama in iambic pentameter. *Pathflower* (1914) came a decade later—a book of lyrics which contained many poems about the North Carolina mountain people. *The Cycle's Rim* (1916), a sequence of fifty-three sonnets on the death of her husband drowned at sea, won a prize for the best book of the year by a Southern writer. *Lute and Furrow* (1922) extended the thematic material introduced in *Pathflower*. Then, for a long while, she wrote no more poetry, convinced that with prose fiction her message could reach a wider audience. Yet poetry was never far away; and *The Spotted Hawk* (1958), which won the Roanoke-Chowan Award, proved that her lyric gift was as intent as ever.

Born in Kentucky, she moved with her school-teaching parents into Missouri and Arkansas. When only thirteen, she assisted them in the classroom. Eager for further education herself, she won a competitive examination and was given a scholarship to Peabody. Before the opening of college, she went on a camping trip to the North Carolina mountains. "If I ever have a home of my own," she said, "it will be in these mountains." Nor did she forget her words during the years she studied and taught and worked at Radcliffe College, in Texas, Nova Scotia, Boston, and New York. In 1906, eight years after her marriage to Pegram Dargan, a South Carolinian whom she had met when he was a senior at Harvard, the couple purchased a farm near Bryson City. The mountain people became her world, and she became their spokesman and has remained so, in spite of lengthy trips to Europe, the death of her husband, and the burning of her farm house in 1923. In 1925, Mrs. Dargan settled in West Asheville, where, at Bluebonnet Lodge, she tends her flower garden when not busy writing. Her fifteenth book, a collection of short stories titled *Innocent Bigamy*, was published in October, 1962.

The theme of Mrs. Dargan's stories and poems may perhaps be described as humanitarian. She believes in Man's unbending spirit which neither confusion nor oppression nor war can destroy. Her poems display a scrupulous, mature technique, and a style and word-choice artfully impressive.

BIRTH

In the Hollow

The hills hover in their snow-shawls
Fringed with black, ragged firs.
In the hollow where three slopes
Touch their great toes together
A hut shrinks down and away
From a cold step-mother sky.
In the hut a woman with gray lips
Sits by a pile of ashes
With now and then a feeble wink
Of fading fire.
Very soon she will be dead;
But on the floor is a screaming baby,
Warm, red, kicking fiercely
With little male feet
At life that gives no welcome.

FAR BUGLES

The mountain road climbed round a cliff,
And there I found him motionless.
Ferns touched his knee, wild columbine rose higher,
And from the moist green ledge above his head
A bunch of crimson water-berries trembled.
I hailed him gaily, one whose gifts to me
Were youth and friendship; but his eyes
Dropped dull as falling birds. I lingered,
Trying to put their light back, and at last
Speech rushed, a voluble wind.

"I'm up an' out by daylight now,
But not to be ahead of the sun
On Katterhay Knob. I've got to plough.
No end at all to the rows an' rows,
I've hardly a minute to look at the crows

That sputter an' nod an' talk together,
Cawkin' that this is plantin' weather
When the corn must go into warm, ploughed ground,
An' in every hill they'll find a grain
I've dropped for *them*. They're tellin' plain
They know their share an' won't take all.
But I don't nod or look around.

Once when I heard a redbird call,
I stood to watch him skewin' up
With the sun a-bubblin' on his wings,
An' makin' my hands like a whistlin' cup
I blew an' called just like he sings.
But old man Gow he rumbled along
An' asked if I wasn't hurtin' the ground
Ploughin' so mighty strong.
He reckoned I'd have enough to pay
The doctor by time the baby come,
If I cut along at a row a day.
Then somethin' more 'bout folks bein' clutter,
An' if my wife was as lazy at home
We'd better move up to the poah-farm now,
An' he'd get a man whose hands weren't butter
When he took aholt of a plough."

 He paused and drew a breath sharp, thin,
Cutting his thought in moody halves;
Then speech came slower, weighed with bits
Of tagging memories, half-born hopes,
And wonders bright and nameless
Dying in his heart.

 "An' Emmie, I don't know her now.
She works an' sews, as busy as me
In the long field rows.
Of mornin's before I go
She gets the breakfast an' milks the cow,
Then hurries to sweep an' make the bed
So she can sit an' sew.

Her hair is tight around her head,
Like crinkled ropes, 'cause her mother grinned,
An' hinted an' sniffed till she had it pinned,
An' I wish she never had come about;
For Emmie's hair when she let it fly
Made me think of the yellow rye
When a July storm comes quick an' the wind
Blows it backward up the hill.
It's queer to see it smooth and still,
Though it's shiny yet as a sleepy trout.
She says it's got to be out of the way,
With much to do an' more ahead,
An' a lookin' glass won't earn our bread.

When I hurry home at the end of a day
She hands me the bucket an' I start for the spring,
But I'm not more than halfway back
Thinkin' I'll clear my throat an' sing,
When she calls to know if the mare's been fed,
'There's wood to get, an' fodder to pack
Out o' that leaky shed.'
An' when at last I get to a chair
I don't believe she knows I'm there.
In a twinkle, it seems, our supper is on,
The kettle steamin', the bread nigh done.
She flashes an' flies like a little gold bee
Till there's twenty women about the stove,
An' strangers all to me.

But when she's asleep she's the Emmie I love;
Paler a lot than she used to be;
Her hair all down an' tumbled bright
In the moonlight dropped like a wispy cloth
Through the window on her; it don't seem right
For me to look, no more'n a thief.
Her eyelids are soft as a white shut moth,
I know if I touched 'em they'd feel like silk;
But I wouldn't wake her, no, I'd as lief

Hit her almost. In sleep, they say,
She's makin' the baby's milk.
An' I'm too tired to watch for long,
So I turn my face away from the moon,
To shut my eyes an' think o' the song
I made for her on Katterhay,
An' sleep an' dream we'll be married soon."

The light was there now, in his eyes
Like gathered, golden blades.
Above him in a gust the berries swayed
As vivid as his lips; and from a heart too full
To close its door, his song pitched out
Leaving the air a passion.

> *Girl I love, girl I love,*
> *Do not stand in the meadow!*
> *A stranger may break*
> *The stem of your body*
> *An' set in his nosegay*
> *Your head's honey-blossom.*

> *Girl I love, girl I love,*
> *Do not lean by the water!*
> *You may fall to the stream,*
> *An' how shall I find you*
> *An' know which is mine*
> *Among the floatin' lilies?*

The berries trembled downward to his hair
As if an elf hand moved them. The stream,
With sparkle and babble, reached for his feet;
But he was still. "She liked the song, Karl?"
Then, out of deam:
    "Ay, ay, she liked it well.
An' all that flutterin' day,
Walkin' beside me, she was like a bell
About to ring, but not a thing she'd say.

Each time she took my hand I felt she'd laid
A young bird in it, warm an' not afraid.
My heart was like a windy tree
Full of little leaves. Right now I see,
With my eyes shut, each turn an' crook
In the trial that day, an' I'd want to die
If I couldn't remember every step we took.
But I reckon Emmie has forgot.
This mornin' she lay asleep, the sky
All pink about her. It wouldn't be wrong
To make her dream of me, I thought;
And with half my breath I sang our song.
Just a whisper it was, but up she flew
With 'My, it's late, an' what's to do;
You oughta been out by good daybreak:'
A shiftless daddy she's sure I'd make,
The dear little thing would starve, she knew!

"When I got to the field I couldn't think.
My heart was hot an' burnin' black.
'Way up in the brush I heard the bleat
Of a little lost lamb, an' I didn't go
To put it right. I saw the pink
Of sarvis buds at the end of a row,
And felt they were bloomin' wild an' sweet
In a world I didn't know.
I thought o' the woods where I used to track;
Moonfeather falls an' the leanin' ash;
The three blue springs where the raccoons drink,
The long slim lake like a painted sash
Dropped from the sky for the woods to wear;
An' I reckoned how if I went back
That *they* wouldn't know I was there.

"At noon when I stopped to feed the mare
I didn't go in to eat.
I knew that you'd be climbin' up,
An' you always stop by the Drippin' Shelf,

To watch it, same as I do myself;
So I waited here to ask you why
Life's got to be nothin' but work an' sup,
However I turn or try?
Why the sun that shouted, 'Karl, let's go:'
Drags like a coal across the sky,
As tired as me an' achin' slow?
Why the wood is only a shut green door,
An' every day is just one more.
I thought I'd ask you if you knew
What a man that's troubled like me can do?"

No other word there fell.
As one who hears too much is still
As though he had not heard,
I watched his eyes drop listless as at first,
Finding no help in mine.
Above us a loud bird,
High in a swinging vine,
Sang resolute, as if the lid
Of some vast trouble pot had burst
Beneath his startled throat,
And he must sound alarm with not one muted note.
I moved to where the bloom
Of a haw bush splashed and hid
My silence from the throttling gloom
About the boy; then slowly found my road,
Taking, and leaving, the old imponderable load.

GUEST ROOM

I've guests tonight in my house,
My wee, my warm and dry house,
Where I take beggars in,
There's Love-too-much, and Cry-I-must,
There's Pray-for-me, and Die-I-must,
And little ragged Sin,
All snuggled up in my house
Like mice in a barley bin.
And it's fine to sit by my wee house door
In cool twilight with milk and crust,
And my beggars all locked in.

HOMEWARD SONG

Again, dear Earth, on flying feet,
I come for board and bed,
Bringing my famished days to eat
Of your unfailing bread.

Almost too late, and not too late,
Your waiting roads I see,
Like host that greets one laggard yet
Your far gates smile to me.

My great beloved, the dust you wear
Is sweet upon my shoe;
Then what of leaves and winnowed air
About the hills of you?

I would be near as grass is near,
Your deep breast fostering,
As near as waters that know where
Your buried fountains sing.

You would I touch, you would I know;
Here take my heart and song;
The fireside loves too soon must go,
But you will clasp me long.

MORNING WINDOW

Dawn! And I fled
From a night without sleep
On a thought-crowded bed.
I would sit by the window, face to the east,
Losing myself, if I could,
Climbing the gold-tipped mountains so still
In the high horizon blue.
They were there, I knew,
But my eyes could not find them,
Could not gather their quiet
Into my heart. I was caught
In the clinging dark
Of a night kept chill with fear;
Fear for a reeling mother earth,
Thrust by witless overgrown power
An inch of time from the brink
Of the black death-jawed abyss.
I could only think of the inch of time,
And wait . . . wait . . . to hear
The fiery crash into nothingness.

Crystaling suddenly
Out of the empty air,
Two cardinals noiseless dropped
To my crumb-strewn balcony.
Beauty alive! And I could see!
Plainly a wedded pair.
She, modest in Quaker gray,
And faintly flushed rosebreast;
He, gleaming in royal red
Marked dashingly
With polished ebon tie,
And prideful crest
Perked toward my eager eye,
As I interpreted
The easy toss that said,

"We do not steal this morning meal,
We know when a welcome board is spread."

They hopped and ate in the late-hung dawn,
Darted and quivered in new-risen sun,
And did they guess how they had drawn
Me out of fearful weariness?
Had given me sight, and a friendly share
In their game of nipping and necking
In unabashed caress?
We three at home
In comradery untouched by doom?

Pausing as though my thought was heard
They gave me an instant of their eyes,
Their keen flash-lidded eyes.
Keen . . . deep . . . deep . . . Yes, it was true;
Deep with reptile knowledge born
Of aeons on the ground;
Ever fearing, ever fleeing
Peril on the ground;
Through flow of ages yearning
To rise on the bosom of air
By no fear bound.

In them urge of the nameless seed,
Invisible save to the Builder of Life,
Sown to the testing fields and waters
Of an answering earth.
Unseen, infinitesimal,
Yet primed with power that gave a world
Its bloom and breath, and moved
With song of flight in surging veins
Till tenants of the ground became
Winged coursers of the air.

Great was your triumph, little birds,
And the torch of undefeat

That no cosmic storm could drive
From your small, deep eyes,
Has cast a darting light for me
On a greater hap of creation
By time's unerring script set clear
In a yet untotaled ledger.

Score of a bolder journey
Under the sleepless watch of the Builder;
The urging seed prodding gestative life
On daring, untried roads
To conscious mind; conscious of self,
Knowing its power, fostering over earth
The multiple race called Man.

Man, with indwelling mind
His servitor, in splendor's passage rising
From tier to tier of knowledge, sun to sun,
Shedding careless brilliance on the graves
Of creeds outlived and gods unmourned.

Man, with thinking eyes
Piercing the core of miracles,
Startling hidden reality to spur
His daily need to know.
The sealed incredibles
Of Nature's morning
Opened to his siege on siege, and fed
His ferreting hunger,
Yielding him food of truth
For wisdom's evening bread.

Triumph on triumph behind him,
Proof on proof of victory
Beyond the farthest sight of seers,
Or reach of prophesy.
Dreamer traversing space

On mind-made wings,
Flashing his ships among stars.

Challenger of doom
Through eras of assault,
How could I sit in blindness,
In shuddering fear believing
You of yourself would choose surrender,
Burying the human world which is you?
How could I see you a reasonless
Tinkering tyrant of force
Who would spread demonic fire
Till a planet embered out?

Come quickly, Magian Man!
This is your time—not Death's;
Time of birth-singing triumph,
Birth of spirit risen in you
To bind the unleashed forces of life
Into insuperable power,
A brotherhood of power
Erasing the pestilent trails
Of ignorance, disease and war
From the shining face of earth.

Quickly, Magian Man; come,
And we can forget the inch of time
On the edge of perdition.
Come with the heart of an earth-wide race,
Your breath the breath of nations,
The breath of love that is life,
Of peace, with far-blown fragrances
To cover the lands and river-fed seas.
Come to the homes where infancy cradles
The safe and holier future.
The past we might bear to lose,
But not the wonders prisoned in time,
Waiting the sound of your opening keys.

You will be true,
Multi-membered Man,
Millions, billions true,
And I, a humble part of you,
Vow you my faith. A faith
That never shall pale to a grave
In the cemetery of doubt.
The world you have mightily won
You will mightily, wisely save
For a long and greater while
Under the nurturing sun
Of the patient Builder's smile.

And if, in far remotest time,
An end must come to all
The great beginnings,
And from a final, flaming sky
The universes fall,
Your own in wisdom's orbit moving
Will be the last to die.

Little birds, little birds,
Who would not serpents be,
Who won the sky nor lost your earth,
Here fluffing and preening to go
To a nest in a tall green tree,
You twinkle me thanks, but what do I owe
For a world returned to me?

PAUL BARTLETT

BY PROFESSION an artist, Paul Bartlett has nevertheless written poetry practically all his life. In earlier days, he contributed light verse, mostly limericks, to the old *Life* magazine. Nor has he quite stopped writing them, as evinced by a recent one on being a poet:

> Said a poet, "It's certainly galling
> To engage in so thankless a calling.
>   As a noble profession,
>   It leads the procession;
> As a business it's simply appalling."

Delightful as such lines are, Paul Bartlett is now primarily a sonneteer, that is, when he is not engaged in painting and teaching.

He was born July 8, 1881, in Taunton, Massachusetts. After Phillips Exeter Academy and Harvard, where he was president of the Harvard Lampoon, he studied art in Chicago and Paris. For a year before World War I, he was American vice counsel in St. Petersburg (now Leningrad). The prizes and honors he won in the art world are numerous. During the decade 1934-44 he lived in Connecticut in the summer and Florida in the winter. On his way south in 1944, he was delayed in Charlotte because of gasoline rationing. There, at the suggestion of a friend, he took a job teaching at the Mint Museum of Art. The following year he was married to Kathleen Bain, an English-born widow who had remained in Charlotte after the death of her first husband. For the next fourteen years, Paul and Kathleen Bartlett were active in the literary and art circles of Charlotte. Then in 1959 the two moved to Guilford College, when Mrs. Bartlett was invited to teach geology and meteorology. Her husband formed classes in the Greensboro area, and continued to paint.

Both of his books—*Moods and Memories* (1957), which won the Roanoke-Chowan Award for a distinguished volume by a North Carolina resident, and *And What of Spring?* (1962), which was illustrated with reproductions of his paintings—are obviously the poetry of an artist whose concern is for contrast, color, and form.

APOLOGY

He dwelt within the hills beyond the town,
    This keeper of a little crossroads store—
A native-son of trival renown
    Where he was born some sixty years before.

The mother, never wed, who gave him birth
    Had struggled with a valiance through the years,
Unmindful of the snickering male mirth,
    Or of the women's surreptitious sneers.

They lived unto themselves, this branded pair,
    Nor ever left their valley's meager site,
And he, alone, continued living there
    When she had gone to death's more kindly night.

Not till he died did neighbors make amends—
They sent a wreath inscribed FROM LOVING FRIENDS.

FINALE

Stupendous are the works of man! Behold
    Vast edifices rising to the sky;
Great rocket-wings wherewith the mortal bold
    May even sound's velocity defy!

Now flowers the epoch of the whirring wheel;
    The wondrous age of mechanistic feats,
When man, the puny one, by steam and steel
    With forces of the very gods competes.

And witness how, with cryptic elements
    Transcending far the violence of thunder,
This marvel of inventive eminence
    Has sired a thing to blast his world asunder!

So, time were better spent composing sonnets
Concerning Spring—or love—or ladies' bonnets.

LESE MAJESTE

Because of its profusion, some profess
   To class wild carrot as of lowly breed.
This teeming Queen Anne's lace is, nonetheless—
   To say the very least—a regal weed.

Its multifloral whiteness, with a trace
   Of coloring from tiny stems of green,
Would surely, in its delicacy, grace
   The bodice or the sleeve of any queen.

Associated thus, the humbly-born
   Partake of royal pridefulness and power.
However, certain commoners would scorn
   The thought that Anne was honoring the flower.

Indeed, they might ungraciously concur
In claiming that the flower had honored *her*.

CITY RAIN

From out the dark, where blurs the buildings' height,
   With falcon-swiftness swoops the city rain.
   No sodden gloom is this of country lane,
Of fields that cringe beneath the tempest's might,
For golden are the windows of the night,
   While, mirrored in the flooded street, each pane,
   Of storm's bedimming flaunting its disdain,
Becomes a reeling reveler of light.

And other gleams, fantastic in array,
   Submerged within the torrent, serpent-lithe,
With flashing undulations now portray
   Such wraiths as in a moonlit river writhe.
Thus, magical, from storm's grim, leaden gray
   Flares forth this transmutation bright and blithe.

LOVE'S ENDING

How love came to an end, I do not know,
    Nor why. It stayed a time, and then passed on.
It was a rippling which, when breezes blow,
    Skims fast along lake's surface, and is gone.

It was the first, fresh blossoming of May
    That lifts its branching splendor to the sky.
And at the morrow is no more. Away,
    And that is all. There was no reason why.

Mysterious, love came, then vanished quite,
    As does the phantom image of a dream.
It was the day that blends into the night.
    It was a leaf that falls upon a stream.

I know not why love went away, nor how.
It was—for but a while, and is not now.

SO INDEPENDENTLY THE CEDARS GROW

So independently the cedars grow!
    Green-dark against the browning pastureland,
    In isolated singleness they stand,
As if each, self-sufficient, scorned to know
Its neighbor tree; as were each proud to show
    To huddling woods that they, sequestered band
    Of individuals, had sagely planned
A life apart from crowd's imbroglio.

And one—robed to the ground, sedate and tall—
    Is in the semblance of a monk designed,
While others, ranging to the pygmy-small,
    Bring less imposing neophytes to mind.
They stand in solemn straightness, one and all,
    Aloof, though in their meager field confined.

EDITH EARNSHAW

ONCE, in answer to a question, Edith Earnshaw replied, "I suppose that my greatest achievement was in being born in Wake Forest, North Carolina." And it is true that most of her writing reflects the village in which she spent practically all of her life. In spite of frequent trips to Europe and elsewhere, she put into her lines the shady streets, the college buildings, the garden club, and the neighbors—especially the neighbors, who were constantly delighting her and whom she was constantly delighting. Her verses—"I never call them poems," she always said—are filled with enjoyment, with wit, and many of them are, to be truthful, downright funny. Though there are serious stanzas here and there, such as the verses on the yearly Christmas cards she sent to friends, it is the joyous caprice of human pretense and foible which most claims her attention.

She was the last of six daughters (the seventh and eldest child was a son) of Dr. Charles Elisha Taylor, president of Wake Forest at the turn of the century. In 1905 she graduated from Meredith College, a Raleigh institution conveniently located near her beloved home. The year following her return, she married Elliott B. Earnshaw, who after attending the college became bursar there. His wife tried to be idle in the village—the way ladies were expected to be in those days—but her energies required direction. First she assisted the new president in his office, stepping across to her husband's when help was needed; then in 1913 she became the bursar's full-time assistant. The ample, long years passed in poetry and zestfulness. In 1953, a year after her husband's death, she retired. Later, when Wake Forest College moved to Winston-Salem, she remained in the village. In these quiet days, she decided to issue a collection of her favorite poems, most of which had previously appeared in the Raleigh *News and Observer*. Seven months before her death on July 14, 1962, *Verses* (1961) was published.

In a foreword to the book, Gerald Johnson commented that Mrs. Earnshaw was "not, as many contemporary poets seem to be, ashamed to being perfectly sane and perfectly comprehensible." With heart-warming simplicity, her eyes roamed the town and countryside of Wake Forest, animating them with poetic humor.

THEY ROASTED ME INSTEAD

The idea for a sonnet came.
Because it led my thoughts astray
We had a thin-soup dinner. I
Forgot to roast the beef today.

I read my sonnet to the folks
Over the soup. Likely as not
They'd say they liked the lines so much
They thought the roast was well forgot.

I thought my sonnet pretty fine
And said so, though I seldom boast.
The family clammed up, then moaned:
"Next time, you'd better cook the roast!"

HE WILL MAKE THE GRADE

Our little Bobby started school today.
We know the peace and quiet cannot last,
But in the house there is the strangest calm
As if a hurricane just hurried past.

"I wonder—will he pass first grade next May,"
His daddy said. I answered: "Sure! I know
They'll pass him! Not a teacher on this earth
Could cope with Bobby two years in a row!"

BABY-SITTER BLUES

Inventing funny games for two active three-year-olds,
  I think the kids well entertained, then Lily
Exclaims in grow-up way, which a lot of boredom
    holds:
  "Betty, isn't baby-sitters silly!"

TWO LITTLE HOUSES

She wrote from England—that new friend I met—
"I have a cottage down in Somerset."
(I too have a house, if she but knew,
In Wake's dear forest, under skies more blue!)
And on she wrote: "You'd like the place, I think;
The roof is thatched; the walls are washed with pink."
(My walls are pinkish brick; my roof is tin—
They keep the weather out; the welcome in.)
"A laughing river hurries past my door;
A nightingale sings in the sycamore."
(A mockingbird sings in my great oak tree,
And in the pines the wind sounds like the sea!)
"My cottage is old England! Do you know
The place was built hundreds of years ago?"
(And fifty years ago mine, if you please,
Was bricks in kilns and living, rustling trees!)
"I greet the cottage with a smiling face
When I go down. Mine is a week-end place."
(Mine is a lifetime place and if I roam
It holds out loving arms when I come home!)

MISS FLO

Miss Flora unfolded red, work-roughened hands
    And said ('twas a bit of a shock):
"My notion of Heaven a long time has been
    Jes' to set on the front po'ch an' rock!"

CAROLINA WRENS

You trill by the treeful!
    I wonder how come
You wake up so gleeful,
    I wake up so glum!

MISS SALLIE'S CHOWCHOW

Cabbage, onions, green tomatoes,
    Peppers, cucumbers chopped small,
Cider-vinegar, brown sugar,
    Mustard, spices one and all—

That's Miss Sallie's famous chowchow.
    She is making it today
And it smells just like delicious
    When the wind blows from that way;

Neighbors passing stop to sniff it,
    Chat beside the paling-fence;
Old Miz Baker told the parson:
    "Sal was born with pickle sense!"

OUCH!

She means it for praise and her motive is pure,
But O, I feel sadly devoid of allure

When best-friend-Olivia tells me that she
Feels perfectly safe when her husband's with me!

PUPPY

He's awfully nosy, that puppy of mine
He heard something wheeze and he heard something
    whine—
Electric fan? Yes! But to him it meant strife,
He never had seen one before in his life!

He went up to smell it, the poor little thing!
(Now puppy is wearing his nose in a sling!)

FADS AND FANCIES

See the motley mass of humans
    Strewn along the beaches,
Plastered o'er with sunburn-lotion
    (Where the sunburn reaches).

Rich man, poor man, beggar, thief, and
    Doctor too and lawyer;
Not to mention injun-chief, and
    Injun's sun-tanned squawyer.

Trunks on shanks like macaroni
    Under beach-umbrellas;
Trunks on shanks mahoganized, on
    Hale and hearty fellas.

Hairy chests and chests of marble,
    Light and heavy chassis,
Heads well thatched or smooth as golf-balls
    —All in dark sun-glasses.

Bathing suits on pretty maidens,
    Pretty suits, just-right ones;
Bathing suits on fat old ladies,
    (Gaudy garments, tight ones).

Plump girl, slim girl, old girl, young girl,
    Plain girl, movie-starlet;
Blistered backs and peeling noses,
    Toes all tipped with scarlet.

Fads and fancies of the beaches!
    To and fro they jerk us;
How the fishes in the ocean
    Must enjoy the circus!

I FELT LIKE SLAPPING HIM

I spent a week in Washington
    And had a lovely time. In truth,
I felt so gay, so free from care
    Almost I whistled back my youth!

I bought a frisky bright red hat;
    I bought a snappy little suit—
O well, not "little"! Still, I felt
    Quite girlish in it. Kinda cute.

Today I caught a crowded bus.
    Alas! I heard a stranger say:
"Come, Grandma, you can have my seat!
    I may be old myself some day!"

MY OLD MAN

My old man, he nods in his chair sometimes,
    And now and then gets him a nap real deep,
And then when it's over, he always says:
    "Just go right on talking—I ain't asleep!"

Course, that's when the neighbors come in to chat
    Of things that don't int'rest him overmuch
Like babies and ailments and recipes
    Crocheting and patterns and teas and such.

Then after they go he will say: "Now, Hon',
    I never missed even a single word!"
He fooled me that way for a long, long time,
    But now I'm convinced that he can't have heard.

For honest, last Sunday he sat in church,
    And my, but he flustered us all a heap!
Half way through the sermon he said out loud:
    "Just go right on talking—I ain't asleep!"

JUST A BREEZE!

The day the bridge club met with me
   The maid sent word she had the flu
And soot poured down the chimney on
   My costly rug of powder-blue;

A bumblebee stung Adelaide;
   The furnace smoked; the house was cool;
His teacher 'phoned me Bobby was
   A naughty little boy in school;

Great-uncle Zeb arrived by bus;
   The icebox rolls refused to rise;
I scorched my handmade tablecloth;
   I couldn't find the top-score prize.

But when the girls went home that day,
   "We've all been talking," said Louise:
"You make us awful envious—
   You entertain with so much ease!"

WHAT IN THE WORLD!

Little freckled lad with a cheerful grin—
In the fields and woods, how he loves to roam!
Which is quite all right, but we never know
What in the world he will bring back home.

There are fishing worms in my antique vase,
And the sofa is covered with rabbit hair;
And a guest couldn't sit in the dining room
Last night, till a terrapin left her chair!

A toad-frog hopped on my bed at dawn;
In the sink, fancy crayfish go glub-glub;
Now we have to take showers, for sixty-three
Plump tadpoles are using our one bathtub!

I asked today in parental tones:
"Son, what are you hiding behind your back?"
He replied: "Now, Mom, 'tisn't nothing 't all
But a copperhead in a paper sack!"

HE GAVE UP GOLF

"I've giv'n up golf forever, Wife,
   I'm such a hopeless duffer.
O no, I didn't smash my clubs—
   Why make poor golf-clubs suffer?

Here—sell them at your rummage sale!
   The poor can use the money."
Says Butch: "Dad, why not try croquet?"
   It wasn't nice of sonny.

A day went by, three days, a week—
   Flat, flavorless and boresome.
Then Bob called up. "Snap out of it!
   Come back and join the foursome!"

"O Bob, I will! Indeed I will!
   At two o'clock today, with—"
There came a pause. "No, Bob, I can't.
   I have no clubs to play with."

"O yes you have!" his wife exclaimed.
   "It wasn't wrong, now was it,
To hide your golf clubs in the hall,
   In the umbrella closet?

I put them in the same old place,"
   Went on that woman clever,
"Just where I always hide them, when
   You give up golf forever!"

QUERY

She talks without stopping;
She's round as a peach;
Would rhetoric call her
A "figure of speech"?

OLD CHIMNEY

Remote from the broad, humming highroad
   One morning I happened to spy
A chimney without any hearth-fire,
   And daffodils blooming close by.

The farmhouse—or was it a cabin?—
   Had crumbled to dust long ago;
The garden—all gone but these blossoms.
   I suddenly wanted to know

Who planted the bulbs in the first place.
   A bride with a dream? Or an old,
Bent granny with work-roughened fingers,
   Who treasured her flowers like gold?

What pioneer fashioned this chimney
   That stands here, all timeless and sound?
O does he perchance lie asleep in
   Yon family burying ground?

These questions I ask of the breezes;
   The wind brings no answer to me,
But stays in the brooding pine forest
   Evoking a sound like the sea.

I bent down to gather the blossoms—
   Each wistful-eyed gold daffodil—
And then changed my mind, lest the chimney
   Should be even lonelier still.

ZOE KINCAID BROCKMAN

SINCE THE FIRST SALE of a poem at the age of sixteen—it was, incidentally, the year she was married—Zoe Kincaid Brockman has been constantly writing, in both verse and prose. She was born on a farm near Gastonia; her family moved into town when she was six months old. There she attended private school, then graduated from Gastonia High School, later took extension courses from the University of North Carolina. Except for short residences in Charlotte and Spartanburg following her marriage, Mrs. Brockman has lived all her life in Gastonia, most of the time holding the position of woman's editor of the *Gastonia Daily Gazette*. During the years, she has written and published more short stories and poems than she can remember. Awards coming to her as poet and newspaperwoman are numerous. Mrs. Brockman is mother of a daughter, who died in 1934, and a son.

In 1932 she was instrumental in the organization of the North Carolina Poetry Society. Not only was she its first president, but associate editor of its successful monthly, the *North Carolina Poetry Review*. Friends began urging her to issue a volume of her poems, but she had taken to heart the advice of Dr. Edwin Greenlaw, "Don't publish your teething pains." Only after the publication of *A Century of Growth* (1946), a centennial pageant she had been commissioned to write for Gaston County, did she decide the time had come. A year or two were spent going through the rather vast accumulation of poems she had filed away, both published and unpublished, before finally a book was printed. *Heart on My Sleeve* (1951) was an immediate success, going through a second and third printing within a few months—a happy but unusual occurrence for a book from a regional press. Later, a collection of essays, *Unguarded Moments* (1959), was titled from a column she writes for the *Gazette*.

The appeal of Mrs. Brockman's poems is so direct that analysis or critical comment seems unnecessary. Her stanzas are manifestly those of a woman, sensitive and aware. Life is always strange but certain, alternating between happiness and sadness, the two often paradoxically united. For her, traditional values seldom demand innovations of expression.

CONCERNING WINGS

A butterfly was once a worm,
Designed to fly, but first to squirm.
Since this is true, it may be I,
With squirming done, may learn to fly.

IN AN EDITOR'S OFFICE

How would you like bright dreams today,
Sparkling and fresh and new,—
Fragrant blossoms on fragile stems,
Heady and touched with dew?

How would you like gay dreams that ride,
Silver and slim and fleet,
On the crest of a sapphire tide
Tuned to a throbbing beat?

How would you like magical dreams,—
Fancies that could come true,
Wrapped in star dust to tease your eyes,
Tied with a cloud's bright blue?

How would you like some minted dreams,
Any old dreams at all?
(Maybe it's dreams the office boy
Is sweeping into the hall).

CARDINAL

One leaf, I thought, has turned bright red,
Autumn has sent a shining word.
And then it turned and skyward fled
To let me know it was a bird.

I SAY TO THE MOUNTAIN

The sky is close to me,
The brook is my friend,
I say to the mountain:
Attend me, attend!

For I from the lowlands
Have need of your peace,
I come to be healed of
The fearful unease

That the earth is a planet
Spinning close to the brink
Of disaster so heinous
No mortal dare think

On what fate may befall him,
What powers could forfend.
I say to the mountain:
Attend me, attend!

A COLD WIND BLOWS

Belovéd, there is nothing I can say
To make pain less or easier to bear,
Our feet are set upon a separate way;
We stumble down a steep, divided stair.
Behind us there are golden days of sun,
Nights when white magic sailed a sea of blue;
Now radiance sinks into oblivion:
A cold wind blows between my heart and you.
But always when blue billows wash the sky,
Always when moonlight spreads an argent sail,
I will remember how both you and I
Strove to withstand a cruel, fateful gale,
And how, defeated, we went down at last
And still must shiver in the eerie blast.

THE DREAM IS NOT ENOUGH

Now that the flesh is gone, there but remains
A fragile dream caught in the lambent air:
Her head against the cushion of a chair,
Her slim, tired form poised in a open door.

The flesh is gone—her temple's loveliness
Locked in the earth, to blossom as a tree
Far years from now. But, oh, again to see
The white lids flutter and the soft lips smile!

The dream remains—her way of looking up
Through curving lashes, and her hand's frail grace
Brushing a wave of bright hair from her face.
The flesh is gone—the dream is not enough!

YOUR FOOTSTEPS ON THE STAIR

Your footsteps, light and hastening,
On oaken stair and wide,
Leave much I must remember,
And much I must decide.

Shall it be a forgetting,—
The iris-colored Spring,
The rainbow-spangled morning,
The moonlit fairy ring?

Or shall I wear aloofness,
A wounded heart to keep,
And tell myself: No, never!
The way too hard, too steep.

Your footsteps, light and hastening,
Make trouble on the stair,
And I, who sought you elsewhere,
Am too aware, aware

Of all your charm and daring,
Your falseness and its lure.
Then stand behind me, Eros,
And I will lock the door.

SORROW'S DAY

Mortgaged to sorrow is this day,
Soft though the mist-blue morning came,
Sun gilds the breeze-stirred ricks of hay,
Birds are calling a name, a name . . . .

Only I know, locked in a moment
Lived through many dark years ago,
This is a day of ache and foment,
This is nadir my heart must know.

After today the world will settle
Back to its old, still way again:
This is the day of thorn and nettle,
This is the day I owe to pain.

CHRISTMAS EVE

A pine branch is so wholesome and so sweet,
I hang a pungent wreath above my door,
(Do angels sing at midnight any more,
And are they heard above the blatant street?)

My string of colored lights is gay and new,
In my small room the tree stands straight and high,
(Is there a special star to light the sky
Whose wintry arch is tranquil and so blue?)

Dear God, there's only tinsel in my hand,
And sprigs of green and little, foolish lights,
(My heart remembers far Judean heights,
And you, I think, will see and understand).

TO THE LOST COLONY

You had been gone so long, and no one knew
Which way you went; but now you have come back.
The ocean's muted organ welcomes you,
Low-growing verdure covers up your track.
And we who read your story long ago,
Who grieved and wondered and gave up the clue
Of "Croatan" carved deep, wait now to know
Just how you lived and spoke when arrows flew
Around your shelter; how you worked and prayed.
We sit around the stage where actors move
The way you moved and shape the words you said;
We know your lives in peace and war and love.
Our printed programs rustle in the breeze
As storied ghosts move soft among the trees.

THREE CINQUAINS

In Winter

The sun
Spills thin gold wine
Upon the earth, and I,
Lifting my lips as if in thirst,
Am warm.

Mountains

Mountains
Press feet of clay
Into the sod—their hands,
Shaping indefinite prayers,
Touch God.

Scissors and Paste

Gold moons
Night after night
Are pasted on blue sky.
Angels, perhaps, pausing in praise,
Play games.

HELEN BEVINGTON

Helen (Smith) Bevington once wrote, "A month or two after I was born on the banks of the Susquehanna, in the village of (flow gently, sweet) Afton, I left the town and the river forever." This was in upper state New York, where she was an only child in a Methodist parsonage. High school days were spent in Hornell, N.Y. Then came undergraduate years at the University of Chicago with a degree in philosophy, later a master's at Columbia with a thesis on Thoreau. Although she had begun a doctorate in eighteenth-century English literature and was teaching at Bedford Academy in New York City, her marriage in 1928 to English professor and specialist in Victorian writers, Merle M. Bevington, plus the arrival of two sons, indicated a change of course. In 1942, Dr. Bevington gave up his position at New York University and came to Duke. There, at a house just beyond Durham, Helen Bevington began to write poetry—all because, she says, "of the particular pleasure of living in the country." Following a year of settling down and writing and experiencing country life after so long a stay in New York, she too began to teach at Duke, where she is now associate professor of English.

Her first poems were brought to the attention of editors at *The New Yorker,* who promptly accepted them for publication and who still have an option on all her work. Her first collection, *Dr. Johnson's Waterfall* (1946), was succeeded by *Nineteen Million Elephants* (1950). Living abroad for a while inspired most of the poems in *A Change of Sky* (1956), which brought her the Roanoke-Chowan Award, as did *When Found, Make a Verse Of* (1961), a writer's commonplace book with her own poems scattered delightfully here and there among excerpts from her favorite authors, and comments on them.

Since hardly a stanza from Mrs. Bevington's pen fails to sparkle with sophistication and wit, she has been all too incautiously labeled a writer of light verse. True as this may be, the statement is still only a half truth. For beneath the excellent good taste and exuberance, a skillful intelligence is seriously at work. Her purpose may be gentle satire, as in her poetic anecdotes on Pepys, Thoreau, and others. Often her voice is that of a Northerner in love with the South, but keenly perceptive. Whatever her purpose, Helen Bevington is always wide awake with enjoyment.

REPORT FROM THE CAROLINAS

It's a debatable land. The winds are variable,
Especially winds of doctrine—though the one
Prevailing breeze is mild, we say, and southerly.
We have a good deal of sun,

And our peach trees bloom too early. The first light promise
Is lightly kept in a Carolina spring
(It blows both hot and cold). Yet by February
There is the flowering

Of yellow jasmine and sudden gold forsythia,
And mockingbirds; at night the threat of snow.
Northerners passing on their way to Florida
Say it's not Florida, though,

This in-between land. There's the coastal region,
For instance, next a calm sea. Yet too near
Are the dangerous shoals, outlying and inhospitable.
One cape is called Cape Fear.

There's the Piedmont, where I live—the plateau uprising
Between high Appalachians and the sea.
It would seem a temperate world. We take our siestas;
Our ways are leisurely;

And people tend to speak to one another,
Observing the civilities. Seldom heard
Is bitter rebel talk now, seldom "Damnyankee,"
At least not as one word.

And everyone is a Democrat, almost,
Though argumentative. Note a few incline
Toward oratory still, being Southern orators.
Our grapes are muscadine.

Our works are amiable. We grow camellias
In Charleston gardens, we raise azalea flowers.
Both the Carolina wren and Whistler's mother
Are specialties of ours.

We have quail in the yard, and dogwood in the woodlands,
A skyful of buzzards, the wisteria trees,
Pines and magnolias. Also we have, lately,
Certain uncertainties —

I speak as a country person—for winds are variable,
Especially of opinion. Watching the land,
We naturally view the weather with misgiving.
We fear for the cotton and

The tobacco crops, for the peach trees worth the saving
From blasting summer drought and freezing springs.
And, being thus concerned with fluctuations,
We fear for other things.

The chances are, one becomes a little provincial,
Too quick to see as a microcosm this
Mid-country where one is, a red-clay country,
An odd antithesis,

Where the apricots flower too soon and the mimosas
Flower endlessly; where now, in the sun-strewn days,
The H-bomb is to flower, in all the seasons —
Another crop to raise.

And nobody says, of the region down by Ellenton,
That winds are gathering there, or that, on the whole,
They threaten ill. Yet, in the imagination,
Fear is another shoal.

SUMMER EXCURSION: SIGNS AND PORTENTS

A gleaming sign in Mystic, Connecticut,
"The Mystic Power Company," gives one a bright
Vision of voltage and a people watt-lit,
But with electric or the inner light?

*

They promise you in Laurinburg, North Carolina,
"Everything for Everybody." But fair
And civic as that offer is of paradise,
I only had a Pepsi-Cola there.

*

"Minnows. Stop Here." Is this a minnow crossing?
And must we wait for whales around the bend?
Stop! Stop for intersections! Stop for Jesus!
Or will the minnows halt us in the end?

*

We are the literate and word-abiding,
Acceptors of the sign. But is it right
To tell us we are passing "Shady Acres,"
When, realtors, there's not a tree in sight?

*

Return, return to Roanoke, Virginia!
The billboards cry to fleeing Cadillac
And Ford and Jaguar. But, being Southern,
They drawl it slightly: "You all hurry back."

*

In Esperance (N.Y.) and Heartsease (N.C.),
The people live in hope, beside the still waters,
And ease of heart—what else can be the answer?—
And pass this talent on to their sons and daughters.

A STREET IN NORTH CAROLINA

My street goes nowhere. A longwinded street,
It takes a while to verify the view
That nowhere really is worth going to

(I live about halfway). You pass my door
On the ride out and back from having been
To what is bona fide, genuine

Nowhere. And it's pine tree in the sun
That bears a notice, weatherstained but neat:
"Speed is checked by radar." Yet my street

Is leisurely enough for tired cats,
Field mice and possums cross it, sleepy-eyed,
Where it relaxes into countryside,

A scattered house or two, the cedar trees,
A clearing, a green river, a stand of pine.
(The white house in the conifers is mine.)

A BOWL OF OCTOBER

October is a breakfast food
With fields of shredded wheat.
The golden cornflakes lie on the lawn,
And wheaties lie in the street.

The puffed rice clouds, the grapenut hills,
Oh! the oatmeal skies, abed
Have wakened me in the crispies air—
And so I have breakfasted.

A WAY OF LOOKING

Some take back February
And with practiced eye
Give it a second try,

In charitable mood, as one
Who born believing ought
Harbors a second thought,

And finds it tolerably
Springlike, as hope should be
On closer scrutiny.

SEPTEMBER WINDS

The day began with water music
And plenty of woodwinds—such an air
As came, you'd say, from an *oboe d'amore*,
Light in tone for a love affair,
Or came from a wailing *flûte d'amour*,
Low in pitch for the overture.

But the sound increased with the river willows
Loudly scraping, weatherblown,
And the brasswinds rose to the squeal of trumpets
And howled with the horns and the deep trombone.
"LOVE!" they blared at the *oboe d'amore*,
The flute, so thin and so amatory.

THE MAGNOLIA BELT

Two stoplights and the Primitive Baptist Church
Take us through the village. Beyond it lies
One hounddog in the road beside one cabin
Beneath two chinaberry trees that rise
Against a skyline—empty otherwise.

FIND OUT MOONSHINE

"Look in the almanac! find out moonshine, find out moonshine."
—Bottom in *A Midsummer Night's Dream*

O Bottom
With the ass's head,
Find out the moon and leave it lit
That I, who have inherited
Its beam and am in need of it,
May be more cautiously aware
Of moonshine in my love affair.

THE NEW LETTER WRITER

"Complete automation comes to letter writing. Now you can write, address, and sign as many as 3,000 letters per hour."—From an advertisement

The trouble is, I hardly know
Intimately, 3,000 people.
At most I've counted 6 or 8,
Which seems a lot, a gracious number,
To whom in letters I might owe
I might with love communicate.

And yet it being in my power
To send at random now epistles
To 30,000? by the day,
To everybody, by the hour,
Vowing my love by automation—
Sweet automatic words to say—

I need but learn the gentle art
Of meaning, 50 times per minute,
The same love letter from my heart
With the same protestation in it
That I am yours, collectively.
So far, the thought depresses me.

JAMES SEXTON LAYTON

Layton's only book, *The Enchanted Garden* (1961), is not quite so fanciful as its title would indicate. All the poems in it, according to the author, try "to face honestly and fearlessly a few of the significant aspects of life that I have encountered in struggling towards the reality of my Self in the clutches of the modern mind." The book is, in brief, a poet's evolving quest.

Further asked to explain his purpose, Layton once wrote: "Looking back, without too considered reflection, I would say that my poems attempt to tell a story, express an idea, reveal an attitude, crystallize a mood, objectify artistically an experience, transform the mask of appearance into the mask of reality, rarefy, condense, and telescope large areas of confused feeling and action into small concentrated, tangible, unified, intelligible segments of strange beautiful revelation.

"In the larger prospectus, in each poem, from a different facet, I try to tell the truth, with restraint, about life as I have experienced it. . . . Drawn together tightly at any time or at any point, life is full of joy and full of pain at the same time, with indescribable tension; but, filtered and refined and shaped into a poem, the experience of life, however painful, loses its terrible contradiction and I am left with an exhilarating sense of freedom. . . .

"When a poem comes, whether on cushioned feet or with noisy urgency, I don't know what it means. I don't know its title, its name, or what it is going to be about. I learn this only by degrees."

James Sexton Layton was born July 4, 1908, in Clayton; he attended school there and at Weaverville. At the University of North Carolina, from which he graduated in 1938 with a major in English, he also received a master's in 1941. Meanwhile he had taken courses in art and philosophy at Duke University. Off and on during the years he had pursued various occupations as diverse as taxidermy and wrestling. After Army service in the European theater, he spent three years with the United Nations in Germany. In 1948, after his marriage in Liverpool to an English native, Dorothy Newall, he returned to North Carolina, settled in Hillsboro, and began to write both fiction and poetry.

CRIME AND PUNISHMENT

An enormous fortress loomed black and grim
Against the morning sky, casting across
The earth a fearful shadow; while inside,
Obsessed with a problem that tore his mind,
Downcast, a kindly warden with kindly eyes
Sat working at his desk, and watched the clock.

He sighed, pressed a button, and sighed again.
The jailor came. "Yes, sir?" the jailor said.
The warden silently looked in the face
Of the man of iron with the fist of the law,
And beyond into some distant tomorrow.
The jailor stood cold. "Yes, sir?" the law said.

"Oh yes!" the kindly warden said at last
In a soft voice, awakened from his gaze.
"It's almost ten o'clock. Has the man's head
Been shaved?" "Yes, sir! Long since!" the jailor said.
"I could see no peace with the man, he wants
It over with. Head shaved, and locked in his cell!"

The warden looked down thoughtfully and deep
Lines came in his forehead. "There is no word
From the governor," he said and shook his head,
And said no more until the walls of the room
Closed in so close that they forced out his thought:
"Commuted, his sentence will never be!"

"The man does not want it commuted, sir,"
The jailor said, stern with face of the law.
"He is alone in the world, he knows no one,
He has no friends; but he has a last request:
He wants his eyes left uncovered, so that
He can look at God when I pull the switch."

The warden nodded. "It's a fine request
And against the rules, but I can't refuse
A man life! Do as he says," the warden said.
The walls of the room drew back and he stood
With his mind relieved. The face of the law
Walked out without a word and closed the door.

The man willingly strapped in the chair winked
And smiled at the jailor to throw the switch,
And as his flesh began to fry, his eyes
Shone with an incandescent fire that split
The universe to the very throne. God raised
His hand to ward off the light, and turned away.

THE ACTOR

The great cathedral stood silent and calm,
Its lofty spires reaching sublimely towards
The sky, as if seeking in supplication
The strength to rise above the things of earth;

While below a throng boisterously gathered,
Shouting and madly waving at a man
Tipping his hat and tottering along
The edge of the wall, high above the rose window.

From the roof top, nearby, beyond one's reach,
A few feet away, his mother and friends
Begged Legro not to waste his talent, begged
Him to come down, not to throw himself away.

And Legro was such a likely young man,
So dashing handsome in his finely cut
Checkerboard suit, his scarlet waistcoat, green
Tie, his black bowler hat and big cigar.

"Please, please, son, come down, please don't!" mother said,
And echoed the police and friends. "Oh, no!
Never!" said Legro. "You'd break my career
Without a bat of your eye, so blind you are!

"Come down, come down, you cry! You don't know who
I am. You're no more than a dozen heads.
Less than that! And look at my crowd below."
And as he pointed down they roared applause.

"Five thousand or more!" Legro said. "And all
The nets and ladders and sirens! Oh, no!
They would be disappointed. And look a-there!
An ash can on the street! My fame is made!"

Like a swan he dived, and hit his mark. Pleased
Indeed had he known, his performance thrilled
The motley throng; leaving the topmost tower
Of the cathedral shorn of counterpoint.

THE LINE OF LIFE

In search of what and where, behind whose tombs
And burning eyes, I came and went to seek
The fate the Sphinx withheld. This round race track,
That never had an end, I ran and ran.

The line of life, a breath, a spring, a stream,
Rising in the hills, tumbled down its slope,
A rocky course, and lost its way among
The sands and a few skeleton remains;
The faithful scythe and serpent then returned,
With their siege of heat, and the friendly sun.

Free, destined or not, I cared not to ask;
The boulders of doubt that rolled up and blocked
The road I kicked aside, and drove ahead
With a new heart, to quell the king of sadness.

VERNON WARD

As one reads the poems of Vernon Ward, the ghost of Walt Whitman crying for universal love in never far away; he is emphatic in his belief "That all love is good/And all hate evil." Even the lines are shortened Whitmanese, the expression frank and easy-going, somewhat stark in its nondependence on imagery. Method is servant to message. Ward would remind us that every man everywhere "feels the warmth of the sun." Wars destroy; it is much better "To kiss than to kill."

He was born in Bethel, March 27, 1913, but attended school in nearby Robersonville, to which his family had moved. There were short periods at Carnegie Institute of Technology and West Point before he graduated from the University of North Carolina in 1935. Since his intention always had been to be a writer, he then set out to gain experience. He taught school, worked in various capacities on a number of farms, became a merchant seaman, and lived briefly in Philadelphia, New York, Liverpool, Paris, and Los Angeles. At one point, on Ocracoke Island, he ran a dance hall and a writers workshop. There have been many other jobs, he says, "working among people of various races, colors, nationalities, and skills, all to the end of being able to write realistically, authentically, and convincingly." Besides two novels yet unpublished because even he views them as too outspoken, his writings include thousands of letters to newspapers on the subject of pacifism and nonviolence in world politics. Once he was state secretary of the North Carolina Socialist Party. For fifteen years, he lived with his wife and two children at Pamlico Beach, where he operated a vacation resort. Then the teaching urge returned and in 1961, after securing a master's degree from East Carolina College, he moved to Chapel Hill to pursue further graduate study in English.

International Poems (1943), privately published pamphlet, was a brave gesture to make in war times. *Of Dust and Stars*, a much longer manuscript, was first issued in 1949 in mimeographed sheets, then in 1958 was brought out in hard covers. Both publications lay bare his life and ideals in warm but unadorned lines. His poems have appeared in many anthologies.

AS YOU ARE, MY FRIEND

If I were a cripple,
As you are, my friend,
I would never see the waterfront
Different than now;
But would sit here at my window,
Day after day,
And see in the distance
The trawlers creeping along
And the tugs drawing their barges by.

If I were a cripple,
As you are, my friend,
I would never walk
Down among the warehouses
And across the railroad tracks
And onto the piers,
Never see the darkies sweating
And rolling cargo,
Or the bilge of ships,
Or by night
The solitary woman
Unobtrusively wearing out her shoe soles.

But all the same
I would sit here at my window,
As you do, my friend,
Seeing the waterfront spread out wide
And washed of its filth.
And I would be happy
Watching the trawlers
Out at sunrise
And in at sunset,
And seeing the sails
Silver by moonlight.

And come stormy weather,
I would paint the fog
With my dreams.

OF DUST AND STARS

Of dust and stars
Man is made,
Of glowing sun
And secret shade,
Of dismal depth
And towering height,
Of weakness faint
And magic might.

Man is made
Of dust and stars,
Of freedom wide
And crippling bars,
Of tender kisses,
Jolts and jars.
A mortal soul
Of stars and dust,
Bound to earth,
Yet rise he must.

Who on earth
Can yet compare
Such potent strength
And frailty rare?
Throughout the stars
What mind could think
A soaring angel
So low could sink?

Body chained,
Head held high,
Feet on earth,
Eyes in the sky.
His finite spirit
Will not fade.
Of dust and stars
Man is made.

TWO CATS MAKE THE WORLD

Two cats at play in the periwinkle,
One attacking and one defending,
Pawing each other caressingly,
Rolling and tossing resiliently,
Skipping and tripping on soft-padded feet.
How wary she is!
Always retreating to be alluring,
Never too far and never too fast,
Always turning to watch his advances.
How sage he is!
Always pursuing and tantalizing,
Never aggressive and never impatient,
Always sure in anxious restraint.

The Empire State rises blue in the morning.
The church-tower bell is just striking six.
The trucks rumble past on their endless mission.
In the periwinkle bed two cats make the world.

MIXED EMOTIONS

About you
For some time
I have had mixed emotions.
Sometimes I have felt,
"I have never loved anyone
More than I love you."

But then, again,
My mood has changed,
And I have felt,
"I have never loved anyone
As I love you."

By now,
I feel the issue must be settled:
"I have never loved anyone
As I love you."

OF VIOLETS

Now
Shall I pause to speak
Of violets
After these eons of struggle?

It was a simple thing:
Today,
A rainy day in April,
I went to milk the cow
In the sparkling rye.
I led her to the edge
Of an ancient wooded graveyard
Where she might find shelter
For the night.
And there I saw the purple,
The violets,
The heart-shaped leaves,
The scalloped blooms
Beneath the budding trees.

As I gathered the scattered violets,
Meaning them for Libby,
I thought of all the years
When violets must have bloomed unseen,
Trampled down by warring men.

If men should die
At the Dardanelles,
Would not the violets bloom?
If atoms showered
The crumbling earth,
Would not the violets bloom?

That faint odor
Of violets
Seems so sweet
Today.

TWO TEACUPS

This morning two teacups
Were on the table,
One from which I had lately drunk
And another.

For quite a while I looked
At the cup across the table.
I picked it up,
Touched its lip to my lip
And caught, I think,
The aroma of a sweeter tea.

The half-cup of tea
Was still warm.
It tasted mildly sweet
And of lemon.
I sipped it slowly.

That was one thing.

Then,
After wandering around the room a bit,
I lay down.

Not my pillow
But the one on the far side of the bed
Attracted me.
I rolled over to it,
Buried my nose in it,
And breathed, I think,
The loveliest perfume.

This morning I did some strange things,
For you had just gone.

HEART PATH

You said,
"A man has to change sometime."
And you were right.
But you meant
Tighten up,
And you were wrong.

If a man is to live
He must *loosen up,*
Free himself,
Be himself.

If man is to know peace,
Each must follow his heart,
Each in his different way.

Love set the path
And made the heart to follow it.

RANDALL JARRELL

POET, CRITIC, NOVELIST, translator, teacher—these words define Randall Jarrell of the Woman's College of the University of North Carolina. He was born in Nashville, Tennessee, on May 4, 1914, spent part of his youth in California, gathered two degrees from Vanderbilt, was on the faculties of several colleges, passed three years in the Army Air Corps in World War II, and served on the staff of a magazine before arriving in Greensboro in 1947 to teach Modern Poetry and Imaginative Writing ("imaginative" because he does not like the word "creative"). There have been leaves of absense: a year as fellow at Princeton, 1951; two years as consultant in poetry at the Library of Congress beginning in 1956. And there have been honors: a Guggenheim Fellowship; membership in the National Institute of Arts and Letters; and the O. Max Gardner Award in 1962 for his "contribution to the welfare of the human race." His second marriage came in 1952 to Mary von Schrader.

Books of poetry are *Blood for a Stranger* (1942), *Little Friend, Little Friend* (1945), *Losses* (1948), *The Seven-League Crutches* (1951), *Selected Poems* (1955), and *The Woman at the Washington Zoo* (1960), the last a National Book Award winner. *Pictures from an Institution* (1954) is a novel. Collections of essays are *Poetry and the Age* (1953) and *A Sad Heart at the Supermarket* (1962). He has a disk in the Yale Series of Recorded Poets. *Randall Jarrell: a Bibliography* (1958) was compiled by Charles M. Adams.

"The poet writes his poem for its own sake," says Jarrell, "for the sake of that order of things in which the poem takes the place that has awaited it." The poem, he insists, must be as plain—or as complex—as its subject. In spite of his international reputation as a master technician, he can be as colloquial as a local-color writer. In the early books, his themes revolved around childhood, literature, and "the pity of war." More recent poems explore man's efforts to attain maturity. It has often been said that Jarrell is one of the most knowledgeable poets of mid-century America: he seems to know everything about all subjects. Yet his poet's voice—sophisticated and often satiric—it never without sympathy. He is well known as a translator, particularly of the poems of Rainer Maria Rilke.

A SICK CHILD

The postman comes when I am still in bed.
"Postman, what do you have for me today?"
I say to him. (But really I'm in bed.)
Then he says—what shall I have him say?

"This letter says that you are president
Of—this word here; it's a republic."
Tell them I can't answer right away.
"It's your duty." No, I'd rather just be sick.

Then he tells me there are letters saying everything
That I can think of that I want for them to say.
I say, "Well, thank you very much. Good-bye."
He is ashamed, and turns and walks away.

If I can think of it, it isn't what I want.
I want . . . I want a ship from some near star
To land in the yard, and beings to come out
And think to me: "So this is where you are!

Come." Except that they won't do.
I thought of them. . . . And yet somewhere there must be
Something that's different from everything.
All that I've never thought of—think of me!

A GIRL IN A LIBRARY

An object among dreams, you sit here with your shoes off
And curl your legs up under you; your eyes
Close for a moment, your face moves toward sleep . . .
You are very human.
                       But my mind, gone out in tenderness,
Shrinks from its object with a thoughtful sigh.
This is a waist the spirit breaks its arm on.
The gods themselves, against you, struggle in vain.
This broad low strong-boned brow; these heavy eyes;
These calves, grown muscular with certainties;

This nose, three medium-sized pink strawberries
—But I exaggerate. In a little you will leave:
I'll hear, half squeal, half shriek, your laugh of greeting—
Then, *decrescendo,* bars of that strange speech
In which each sound sets out to seek each other,
Murders its own father, marries its own mother,
And ends as one grand transcendental vowel.

(Yet for all I know, the Egyptian Helen spoke so.)
As I look, the world contracts around you:
I see Brünnhilde had brown braids and glasses
She used for studying; Salome straight brown bangs,
A calf's brown eyes, and sturdy light-brown limbs
Dusted with cinnamon, an apple-dumpling's . . .
Many a beast has gnawn a leg off and got free,
Many a dolphin curved up from Necessity—
The trap has closed about you, and you sleep.
If someone questioned you, *What doest thou here?*
You'd knit your brows like an orangoutang
(But not so sadly; not so thoughtfully)
And answer with a pure heart, guilelessly:
I'm studying. . . .
                If only you were not!
Assignments,
        recipes,
                the *Official Rulebook*
Of Basketball—ah, let them go; you needn't mind.
The soul has no assignments, neither cooks
Nor referees: it wastes its time.
                It wastes it time.
Here in this enclave there are centuries
For you to waste: the short and narrow stream
Of Life meanders into a thousand valleys
Of all that was, or might have been, or is to be.
The books, just leafed through, whisper endlessly . . .
Yet it is hard. One sees in your blurred eyes
The "uneasy half-soul" Kipling saw in dogs'.
One sees it, in the glass, in one's own eyes.

In rooms alone, in galleries, in libraries,
In tears, in searchings of the heart, in staggering joys
We memorize once more our old creation,
Humanity: with what yawns the unwilling
Flesh puts on its spirit, O my sister!

So many dreams! And not one troubles
Your sleep of life? no self stares shadowily
From these worn hexahedrons, beckoning
With false smiles, tears? . . .
      Meanwhile Tatyana
Larina (gray eyes nickel with the moonlight
That falls through the willows onto Lensky's tomb;
Now young and shy, now old and cold and sure)
Asks, smiling: "But what is she dreaming of, fat thing?"
I answer: She's not fat. She isn't dreaming.
She purrs or laps or runs, all in her sleep;
Believes, awake, that she is beautiful;
She never dreams.
      Those sunrise-colored clouds
Around Man's head—that inconceivable enchantment
From which, at sunset, we come back to life
To find our graves dug, families dead, selves dying:
Of all this, Tanya, she is innocent.
For nineteen years she's faced reality:
They look alike already.
      They say, man wouldn't be
The best thing in this world—and isn't he?—
If he were not too good for it. But she
—She's good enough for it.
      And yet sometimes
Her sturdy form, in its pink strapless formal,
Is as if bathed in moonlight—modulated
Into a form of joy, a Lydian mode;
This wooden Mean's a kind, furred animal
That speaks, in the Wild of things, delighting riddles
To the soul that listens, trusting . . .
      Poor senseless Life:

When, in the last light sleep of dawn, the messenger
Comes with his message, you will not awake.
He'll give his feathery whistle, shake you hard,
You'll look with wide eyes at the dewy yard
And dream, with calm slow factuality:
"Today's Commencement. My bachelor's degree
In Home Ec., my doctorate of philosophy
In Phys. Ed.
             [Tanya, they won't even *scan*]
Are waiting for me. . . ."
                Oh, Tatyana,
The Angel comes: better to squawk like a chicken
Than to say with truth, "But I'm a *good* girl,"
And Meet his Challenge with a last firm strange
Uncomprehending smile; and—then, then!—see
The blind date that has stood you up: your life.
(For all this, if it isn't, perhaps, life,
Has yet, at least, a language of its own
Different from the books'; worse than the books'.)
And yet, the ways we miss our lives are life.
Yet . . . yet . . .
             to have one's life add up to *yet!*

You sigh a shuddering sigh. Tatyana murmurs,
"Don't cry, little peasant"; leaves us with a swift
"Good-bye, good-bye . . . Ah, don't think ill of me . . ."
Your eyes open: you sit here thoughtlessly.

I love you—and yet—and yet—I love you.

Don't cry, little peasant. Sit and dream.
One comes, a finger's width beneath your skin,
To the braided maidens singing as they spin;
There sound the shepherd's pipe, the watchman's rattle
Across the short dark distance of the years.
I am a thought of yours: and yet, you do not think . . .
The firelight of a long, blind, dreaming story
Lingers upon your lips; and I have seen
Firm, fixed forever in your closing eyes,
The Corn King beckoning to his Spring Queen.

SAM RAGAN

IN "SOUTHERN ACCENT," a column Sam Ragan initiated in the Sunday *News and Observer* back in 1948, the poetry of a number of subsequently well-known North Carolina writers has been introduced. The column was and still is a mixture of literary criticism, anecdotes, oddments, commentaries, and poetry. "The discovery and presentation of new writing talent gives me much pleasure," Ragan insists; "and in comment and critical appraisal of the work of both new and established writers of North Carolina and the South, I like to hope I have occasionally given encouragement." So true has this statement been that readers, quite used to Ragan's beating the drum for others, have not realized that he is a poet himself. His work has, even so, been published in a number of poetry magazines and quarterlies, is found in two anthologies, and appears without special by-line in his column.

He was born at Berea (Granville County), December 31, 1915. In high school he became interested in writing and kept this interest up during college years at Atlantic Christian, from which he graduated in 1936. Before going with the *News and Observer* in 1941, he edited weekly papers in Moore and Onslow counties, pursued journalism briefly in Wilmington, Goldsboro, Concord, and San Antonio, Texas. After war service with the Army in the Pacific, he returned to Raleigh, became managing editor of the morning paper, and in 1957 executive editor of both Raleigh dailies. When time permitted, he served as a special lecturer in journalism at North Carolina State College, and for many years conducted a class in contemporary issues there. Ragan has been president of practically every journalism organization in North Carolina; in 1963 he assumed the presidency of the Associated Press Managing Editors Association of America. In 1939 he was married to Marjorie Usher, newspaperwoman and free-lance writer, and has two daughters.

With a freedom of line, and often with a starkness made poetic by concrete images, Sam Ragan's poems often conjure up a North Carolina of several decades ago. Especially would the vignettes seem to depict, with romantic nostalgia, an age now poetically a visualization of sadness and loneliness—a device for which the past is merely a symbol of man's always tragic sense.

GRAY HORIZONS

Sometimes the birds pause in flight
To feed upon the foam-beaten sands
But more often they wheel and cry
Far overhead, never stopping, until night's
Soft crescendo of silence
Calls them home.

The beach is a lonely place
On days like this,
And eyes see far until
The place where sea meets sky
Brings vision back again
To the glitter and cry
Of flashing sea-gulls.

And here is the haven of
Life's mute testimonials—
A broken car, a battered box,
And here the wreckage of some
Mist-shrouded odyssey.
They tell no tales, except silence:
The story is your own.

HIDDEN SCARS

Fire had come to these woods one day,
and left the trees blackened and scarred—
dead in places, too—
with their limbs hanging like the broken wing of a bird.
But they came out of it somehow,
out of the fire, I mean—
and five years, ten years, perhaps,
one would never know of the hidden scars . . .
Unless other fires came.

"THE PROPHET"

He had grown quieter now,
And almost forgotten—
The Prophet
Only comes to town at tobacco-market time,
And he's only moved to preach
When pimply-faced boys snicker
At his long grey beard and high black hat.
He'll roar at them then,
Damnation and spittle directed at their faces.

But there was a time—yes, there was a time—
When they would not have laughed.
There was a time when he stood in the street,
With eyes lifted to an August sun,
And hellfire pouring from his lips,
Throwing their sins out for all to see.
The poor bastards who felt that hell could be no hotter
Than the tobacco rows down which they marched—
But sin was real and damnation sure,
And the Prophet knew where to hit them where it hurt.
He could preach for an hour, two hours, and they would listen,
Scuffing the dirt and never hunting shade
Until the Prophet had poured out his scorn
And walked away.

The old man's fire is gone now,
He dozes in the shade of a mulberry tree
And mumbles to himself, brushing flies from his face—
Hell is far away,
Beyond the cornfield, the cotton patch,
And maybe even beyond the dusty towns of long ago.

A COUNTRY SAGA

They carried him home in late August
And all through the warm days of September
He lay with two broken legs.
Then with the cool nights of October
Came the fever,
And in the haze of the autumn he died.

They buried him in the weed-grown graveyard,
While his father hobbled, dry-eyed, to gaze.
The next day they turned his bed to the sun,
And the smoke of the evening came home to rest.
The old man sat on the porch and smoked.
"It will rain tonight," he said.

DEER HUNT

We rode out to the west of town,
It was November, the leaves were brown,
And the wind was pushing against the pines
That stood at the crest of the hill.
We saw it but made no comment,
The deer was motionless,
There by the side of the road.

We had slowed, watching him,
Wondering the way he would go.
There was the shot, he leaped high
And came to rest on the road's edge. . . .
Down the bank scrambled the men,
Guns cradled in their arms,
And they gathered round,
Not too close, they feared his kick. . . .
But he was dead, and soon they lifted him up
To test his size, his weight, to count his points.
We saw instead his glazed eyes,
Remembered him alive as he stood in our view,
And we drove away.

PORTRAIT

She spoke of things of long ago,
They were as yesterday.
She told of a dream:
It was a September
And it was not really warm until noon.
I had been sitting in the sun, she said.
I could hear a crow across the field,
On the trellis there were new roses.
    I was sitting in the sun,
        And he brought me three fresh pears
            from the tree in the far pasture.

DESERTED HOUSE

He went out at dusk,
    out from the house
that stood beyond the little patch
    of pine, where honeysuckle
    grew along the ground and a large boulder
    reared and around which
    the path circled.
He went out at dusk,
    and there was a whippoorwill's cry
from the dark wood and across the fields
    now broken with October.
Somewhere . . . somewhere. He did not know. . . .
And the woman who saw him go
Knew that he would not be back.
She left the door open
    and night crept in,
    and when she had gone,
    how many days, weeks, or months had gone by. . . .
The sunlight slanted across the floor
And a curious squirrel left tracks in the dust.

HUNGER AND RAIN

It's not quite all merely to be hungry
For hunger can be translated into many languages.
But being hungry—that is wanting something very much
Is one's own personal hunger
To be tied up in concrete things
As food, sleep, love or laughter
And all the many little things
One doesn't think about often.
Not often enough, at any rate, to wonder about them.
Really I can't add them up—even by minute tabulation
I'm sure I would miss a few.
Hungers, you know—like wind and rain in the teeth
Or birds flying high southward, the sun in their faces.
Measuring the little things often takes a long time
And even then it would not be satisfactory
Like an open fire is.
Maybe it all adds up to the place where
Being hungry really doesn't count except for you
It's odd how things work out like that,
That is tying certain knots the same way as
They have always been tied.
And wondering about them while rain
Falls softly on the trees.

THAD STEM, JR.

A RATHER GENERALLY RECOGNIZED FACT is that, while the writing of poetry has its compensations, it is hardly a remunerative occupation. Yet Thaddeus Garland Stem, Jr., considers himself a full-time poet. Poetry, he says, "is the real aim and objective of my life." Because he has a family and must earn a livelihood, he has a job, which by a wisdom of arrangement he has kept separate from his "real aim and objective." For the poet in America, this is the way it must be.

Thad Stem, Jr., was born in Oxford, January 24, 1916, where he has lived all his life. At public and preparatory school, his principal interest was in football, basketball, and baseball—an interest he kept up at Duke University. After service in World War II, he became Veterans Service Officer of his native Granville County. In 1947 he married a widow, Marguerite L. Anderson, now a portrait painter, and acquired a son. Besides writing, his tastes run to history and politics. He was appointed chairman of the State Library Board by Governor Terry Sanford.

His first poems, which he began to write in 1944, appeared shortly in periodicals. *Picture Poems* (1949) exhibited an individual style which has since marked all Stem's work, both poetry and prose. *The Jackknife Horse* (1954) won the Roanoke-Chowan Award. The next two books—*The Perennial Almanac* (1959) and *The Animal Fair* (1960)—were composed of short prose pieces with characteristic poetic overtones. *Penny Whistles and Wild Plums* (1962) presented twenty-eight poems with prose commentary. "These poems and prose pieces," Stem wrote, "have no direct relationship except in a few cases when I have asked the reader to look over my shoulder.... I want the prose to be a projection, an extension from the verses."

The town of Oxford is implicit in every line Stem writes—the quiet shady residential streets, the courthouse, the business district, and the countryside beyond. In an attempt to interpret rural and small-town manners and customs, it is his purpose, he says, "to recolor and vitalize commonplaces, to make them glowing and fresh." To do this, he has had to become an expert in the use of simile and metaphor, so that the reader may feel that the place or character in the poem, though quite familiar, has never quite been seen just that way before.

BLOTTING PAPER

This bedlam is a cracked platter of cold fried eggs,
A dirty shirt with a missing button, and a handful
Of transfer tokens on a defunct trolly-line.

It's uneaten pears rotting on a grimy shelf
A mantlepiece littered with faded photographs, and
A billion bumblebees searching for something to strike.

It's a hangover and buttermilk dark with flies,
A host of lovers sinning behind the hedgerows
To show their contempt for springtime's wayward spice.

But yesterday a fool of a mockingbird came blundering along
Without any passport or any license to sing, blotting up
The loose ink from a million smeary odds and ends.

SURE SIGNS

A rickety wagon lumbers over the hill
Screeching like brand new brogans
And filling the air with scents of axle grease
And green pine wood.

The woodcutter says 'twill be a fine day
But damned if winter soon won't come,
The way the days get shorter and shorter
Like a bookkeeper's pencil.

CHURCH BELL—WINTER TIME

The Methodist bell's got the croup.
You'd think religion a mousy introvert
The way the bell wheezes in the ice and wind.
But I think he's play-acting, feigning Uriah Heep,
Slyly setting a trap to lure the likker-dick lads inside
To crack their sin-soaked, bewildered heads
With his all-atoning clapper.

CRISIS

An old man leading his jackknife horse
Around the fringe of darkening woods,
Mumbling about the accursed wilt
And the wild grass running as ravenously
As a gang of vampires.

The season's terrible, crops are worse,
And idiot papers speak of nebulous troubles
Somewhere off beyond the horizon.
Trouble is it! By God, they ought
To wrestle awhile with downy mildew
That kisses young plants with the lips
Of the devil, himself.

Wonder what's for supper now?
A rasher of fine, lean side meat?
He clucks to his horse excitedly—
Flying sparks from steel on stone
Send fireflies sailing to Hickory Wood.

OLD HUP

Old Hup comes tottering down the street
Leaning on his cane;
He calls to mind a rusty tool
Left standing in the rain.

And all along the village square,
The lads all laugh to see
Old Hup going, God knows where,
On another spree.

I often wonder, my scarecrow friend,
If you recall the times
You picked my Ma wild roses
And courted her with rhymes?

OLD MAN'S FANCY

Love is a hungry hobo
Knocking on back doors
For last night's left-over dreams.

Love is a small boy
Quarantined with chicken-pox, and
Pressing his face against the bedroom window
To look for Robin Hood or for men from Mars.

Very often, love is a cat on a fence
Somewhere after midnight, striking
A yellow paw at moonbeams, and being predatory
In a haughty, hump-backed way
About squatters' rights and all the hosts
Of Johnnies-Come-Lately.
(And as I have observed
Love is also a tall water-lily
Being majestic and unsullied
Above three frogs with boisterous manners).

But principally, love is a hobo
Blowing a ragtime harmonica at kitchen doors
And making chalk marks on the friendly ones
For tomorrow's ravenous minstrel.

COURTHOUSE BELL

The monody, then the cacophony
Tremble out across Settle's Lane,
A giant pendulum suspended by monstrous fate.
It goes slowly at first, like mercy begging,
Then faster, faster, as if justice were a hound
Feverishly pressing a spending fox.

SOMETHING MORE

Beauty is something more than a sky, a bird, a field,
Or the ripple of wind in wheat, or the autumn luster,
Or a mountain's leafy fingers pulling grapes
From a blue cloud cluster,
Or the wonder an artist sees
In river or trees.

Beauty is something more than the peace when old friends meet
On a village street,
More than the sounds that day has sweetly laid
In the night's shade.

I think beauty must be the heart's own token
That gentleness outlasts all wrongs and wars,
That the strong heart wins over at last by softness
All the mind abhors.

SCHOOL DAYS

He knew he had the place alone
And he'd better find out who was puttering
Around the wood pile and singing such
A sad, sad song.

It was only the wind out there
Playing a made-up game of bloodhound,
Sniffing the chips and fallen leaves,
A forgotten child playing by himself,
Poking through the hedgerows just to see
How the other side would look.

For all the apple green was gone,
And all the blue and pink and gold, and
The wind being left alone had to improvise.
You know, like a five-year-old in early Fall
When everyone's gone to school.

MAN RAKING LEAVES

I saw a man raking leaves
And I asked if he raked to rid
The grass of suffocation, or if
It was merely the time and season for raking?
And if it was purely a matter of personal importance,
Perhaps it was to get the steaming bottom leaves
To toss at Spring as furtive calling cards.

But he said he was passing time without a watch,
The same as men scrawling aimless verse or bandaging toes
Or speaking to a jury, or catching fish,
Or singing a love song in tune. Just so.

PAGING PROFESSOR GOOSEBERRY

When Professor Gooseberry gave up his ghost
He laid down his bow. His palsied hands
Had already dropped his fiddle. The funeral
Was the biggest thing since the opera house fire,
And we brought him where
The wind was sweet on April air
Because a strong element of poetry was implied.
But it was a toss of a fiddle string for top billing
Between dozens of cousins and lodge hall buddies
And assorted colleagues. (Not to mention Gooseberry.)
Everybody who didn't make a speech had a part, and
There was enough respectful commotion to make
The wind crawl into the church mouse's hole.
But what I am morbidly curious about, and
I really wish someone would tell me: Is there
Ever any balm for fiddlers in any new Gilead,
Or does everyone, Gooseberry included,
Have to try out for a harp, if only for size?

DEEP SUMMER, AFTER MIDNIGHT

The town's fast asleep as a child spent from play.
Streets are trundle beds under darkest counterpanes,
And down the deep well of a cobbled alley a restive horse
Beats a cloppity-clop requiem for zooming bees
And leapfrog games and pretty maidens, not in a row.
The echoes are a flood of question marks
Spending wantonly among the eaves.

There's hardly a whir among the linden trees
Where the wind tips on furtive toes, but Howard's rooster's
Suddenly louder than thunder on a fiddle string. If one
Didn't know better, one'd think this officious fowl
Is apostrophizing the little brown hen that loved virtue
More than lethal cars in heavy street crossings.
(If not she was a scenery-loving little missionary
That leaped where her sisters feared to tread.)

BOY ON THE BACK OF A WAGON

I doubt he even bothers to suspect this world
May soon be claimed by fire. His legs dangle
From the rear and keep time to the slow rolling
Of the shuffling wheels. Now it's queer
He should have troubled to hail the wagon
When legs would do the distance to the creek
In almost half the wagon's time.

      Well, perhaps he holds it true
That prolonging the journey enhances the final joy?
Or maybe it's just to see the wiggling road behind him
Crawling around the green trees like an apathetic snake?
Or is it he blows his harp better sitting down
And can fuller serenade the crows this way?

But he didn't ask me to explain what needs explanation
No more than wild blackberries need sugar and cream.
I think he rides simply because he's going somewhere
And the slower the ride, the sweeter the trip.
The creek is merely a station at the end of the line
And the day is redolently precious with spice and mint,
And he senses something indecorous in plunging headlong,
Though he's not so smug a fool to go hunting reasons
For riding slowly through Maytime's secret heart.

POST CARD

Old Mr. Hobson's gone to Florida,
And somebody in town ought to write him
His woods are drowzy as an old lady
Cat-napping before a peevish fire.
Cold stars are candles much too brief
To light the way to long, long dreams,
But the last bird sings agonized requiems
For all those blue-green oddments moulding
In April's musty album. And Mr. Hobson's woods
Are drowzy as an old lady, shorn of appetite,
With nothing left to wait for but the supper bell.
Now, if I had the talent (I mean if I hadn't
Had to go to work in the fifth grade,—somehow
It's always clearer, neater, put that way),—
I'd send Mr. Hobson word that a lady in a pink coat
Came hurtling down the turnpike, and her horse's mane
Tossed foaming sleet that cowered Mr. Hobson's woods.
Yes, sirs, I'd write him word
A lady in a pink coat
Came riding hard to hounds,
Lickity-split along the turnpike,
And Old Mr. Hobson's woods
Haven't stopped playing dead-dog yet.

LITTLE SAUCERS, BIG SAUCERS

Beyond any doubt (and you can add "peradventure," too)
You'll admit you've heard your blood brother creek
Cursing himself for stumbling on submerged logs,
And you've watched him take a grade wearing maple leaf
In his hat and calling himself a mountain climber. (And
Never mind the adult dunces who are just bound to prattle
About up hill and down hill and such gravitational junk.)

And give me the telephone number of anyone
Who has never heard redbuds telling Friday morning
About spruce trees that think they're fat landlords
Tapping their bellies and telling each other how
There hasn't been such a season for growing
Since Bryan and the Chautauqua came to town.

And who, do pray tell, has not seen the wind
Sit cross-legged in a circle of sedate water lilies
To shock these prim sisters to chalky embarrassment
With ribald ballads from across the sea?
If such an idiot should deign to speak
He cannot hold forth in this piece.

CHARLES EDWARD EATON

ONE CAN BELIEVE that Charles Edward Eaton spends a good part of every day in the composition of poetry. Even to list his contributions to periodicals would require a lengthy bibliography. Yet he has been deliberately slow to bring out his poems in book form. *The Bright Plain* (1942) made promises fully redeemed in *The Shadow of the Swimmer* (1951), winner of the Ridgely Torrence Memorial Award presented by the Poetry Society of America for a distinguished book of lyric poetry. Critics noted that the book was no mere collection of stray poems by one author, but a group solidly bound together by a dominant theme. *The Greenhouse in the Garden* (1956) was one of the candidates for the National Book Award in poetry. *Countermoves* (1962) was published simultaneously in Canada, England, and the United States. *Write Me from Rio* (1959) is a book of Eaton's short stories.

He was born June 25, 1916, in Winston-Salem. At the University of North Carolina, from which he graduated in 1936, he wrote plays for the Carolina Playmakers. After a year of graduate work at Princeton, he taught English at Ponce, Puerto Rico. From 1938 to 1940 he was at Harvard getting a master's degree, after which he taught creative writing at the University of Missouri. As Vice Consul at Rio de Janeiro, he spent four impressive years in Brazil during the war, then in 1946 returned to Chapel Hill to resume his teaching career. He was married to Isabel Patterson of Pittsburgh in 1950, and two years later, after giving up teaching, moved to Woodbury, Connecticut, to devote his entire time to writing. Even so, Charles Edward Eaton never was long away from North Carolina. He returned frequently to visit friends and relatives, and finally in 1961 bought a house in Chapel Hill where he and his wife spent winters and springs.

"I am neither a romanticist nor a classicist (difficult labels!)," Eaton once wrote, "but prefer to think of one as the correction of the other and to look towards *wholeness*, recognizing both expansiveness and restraint." Beyond labels, Eaton's poetry—always full of color and sensuousness—states forcefully the dichotomic oppositions in nature: for example, the duality of life and death. Darkness and decay haunt that which is most beautiful; one must guard against artificiality. Through poetry, the discovery of reality is possible.

CAROL

Here's a wreath of Christmas holly,
Thorny green and blood-red berry;
Touch of it is scourge of folly,
Watch it only and be merry.

Tear the flesh, remember Jesus,
Feel the panic in the finger;
Hearty carol can't redeem us
Unless an angel were the singer.

Ardent circle others fashion
Cannot crown our faint endeavor;
We must thrust the hand in passion,
Thorn and berry, twine together.

Here's a wreath of Christmas holly,
Thorny green and blood-red berry;
Touch of it is scourge of folly,
Watch it only and be merry.

THE COMPLEAT SWIMMER

Divers are like insertions, incisions, when they fall.
They have the confidence of all the years of man
The golden weight will be received, that they can
Enter an element not their own without reprisal.

Their muscular, ruthless plunge would say:
Longer than any other we have remembered passive blue;
The tingling seduction goes back to that first day we knew
Invasion, in all probability, would be our way,

The clean thrust in the sun, repeated *ad infinitum*—
Do not we who did our share of diving long ago,
Until it faded like an act of love, still know
When the golden dagger flashes in a murky room?

Overhead, the beautiful, savage play, and, here, the other role
Of seasoned helper in a magic act
Where knives seem to enter but in fact
Do very little damage to the unimpassioned soul.

THE WAVES

Now it is here, the summer's richness, poised like a wave.
All spring the green was rising, tidal with unrest—
Now sound of trees is like the flowing toward a crest:
In such an imminence you do not know what you should save.

Along every passage followed, the green hangs over
From bank and bough, and if it fell the thud
Would take along with all confusion what most you loved and understood—
Nature never winnows from the flesh the thinker and the lover.

At night the scent of honeysuckle flows across your bed
In currents that awaken body to the body's love;
If for a moment you protest, resist, the shove
Of opulence thrusts reason under like the swimmer's head.

And you must learn desire can be a way of dying, as though even
The eaves of the world were waves dark with threat
To any truth affirmed and every beauty met,
Holding precarious to summer earth the curve of heaven.

CREPE MYRTLE

This is the myrtle of the South,
Creped and colored like the watermelon's inner flesh.
It burns the oil of branches, and, in the dry wind-thresh,
Ignites the air of August, month of wasted summer
    and of drouth.

The sweating florid faces look ready to explode:
They, too, from the same earth. They, too, from
    the same earth.
In the blazing prism of afternoon, death and birth
Touch but never fuse with the eternity of the road.

The myrtle and hot faces in the brazen air,
By suction from the green, from the wax-melting flesh,
    with love or lust,
Bloom, surge, and throb what will not be the dust
Until the white and phantom road is not and never
    will be there.

COPPERHEAD

We swerve to arousal: the trembling man fanged by a
    copperhead,
The human whiteness that looked unclean when it was struck.
Carried home in rage and fever, with luck
He lives. With another kind of luck he will soon be dead.

Who could have thought a dignity when he blanched,
    leapt back, unnerved,
Suddenly loosely open, vulnerable, nowhere whole,
As though it were not flesh but the utterly helpless soul
Awaiting the bolt of venom like damnation it deserved?

Somewhere in the grass the reptilian radiance is moving free,
Heating our terror, ruthless as any dominant skill;
The weakness of our love pursues the brown entity of pure
    evil,

Seeking a firmness that could foil the failure of integrity.

It was the flimsy answer, the contemptible shoddiness, that
 made us cower,
The flesh swaddling good and wrong, lacking all coherence
 that could act,
While fate had kept the function of our ancient enemy
 compact,
Poison-clean, lightning-swift in power.

With passion's gravest error, we saw them equal in a time
 and place,
Thought of the brown king as braver and more rightly
 proud than we,
And there was nothing could make us see under the looming
 aura of eternity
The blent and possible man, more beautiful than evil's
 purity, destruction's grace.

A LOVE-DEATH STORY

Under the tulip tree in white
She sat, under the purple-rose,
Reading the love-death story
Full of foreign names and evening light—
Dressed for springtime, white and cool.
I knew that if I spoke or chose
To take her hand, I would presume upon the glory
Of her dominion under violet rule.

But why should carnal hand delay
Unless her whiteness were a cause for terror?
At the moment of the suicide,
If I should speak, would she look terrified
That there were anything to say,
That I should think that love in error?
In silence, I was prisoner, loyal
To realm of rose and purple royal.

She saw the world I stood in at a glance,
Beyond the circle of illusion,
And never yielding from romance,
Nor granting, nor forbidding, my intrusion,
She never knew I saw her white,
Nor knew I loved her in that light,
And wished, in truth, all flowers were unfurled
Somewhere, for her, in purple world.

IN THE HEADLIGHTS

Over and over, the staring owl remembers not to blink.
Swerving toward him, my car at night makes stolid jewels of
    his eyes,
And I remember suddenly that gods may never wink.

A quick totem, a flash across the mind of some tabu,
And braceleted, rainbowed deep into my flesh with hidden
    hero's wishes,
I rush on across the night, some other one I knew.

That bird, burning only in his eyes,
Gives me quicker than a crime all the swag
Of someone running out on paradise.

I see him, just that moment, at the turning of the road,
A confrontation like a power I had long since carved
And set down at this secret place when I should need a god.

Not many have the danger and the pleasure
Of rushing jewels into morning. Such escape
Goes dull as dead men's eyes when we recount its virile glance
    at leisure.

But then what god ever was only a bird of prey?—
There will be moments by quiet streams when, without us,
    time flows on forever,
And vague, diffused plurality may be the fate those eyes
    intended to convey.

NOTES FOR AN AUTOBIOGRAPHY

Hardly thinking of years, but sensing their flow, again
I mate with lilacs—the unimpoverished kiss—
Whispering, mortality is the maker of men.

What clings to us, what sticks, what makes tattoo?
I was a joyous and a tragic child—
From images, well-savored, I at last outgrew
The taint of all things blandly reconciled:
I am both provident and wild.

This earliest, perhaps pre-sexual, image—a boy bending over
The little huddled town of purple-blue, spired for worship:
It stuck to me, it clings to me, compulsive as a lover.

Now friends ask, knowing something of my age,
As though what lives could ever quite deny the womb,
How and when, so vulnerable to image,
I blessed my ancestors in their tomb
And looked upon the world with more aplomb.

I boggle at a forthright answer. I prefer
To show my hand beneath the bush, surprise them with delay,
While in the varied, erratic light, birthmarks shift and blur.

FRANK BORDEN HANES

THE POET AND NOVELIST Frank Borden Hanes was born in Winston-Salem, January 21, 1920. He went to local schools and Woodbury Forest. There were occasional vacations in Montana, which has provided the background for two of his books. The year 1942 was a banner one: he graduated from the University of North Carolina, was married, and became an ensign in the United States Navy. Oddly enough, it was in the Pacific, where he participated in actions at Guam and elsewhere, that he first began to write poems, most of them about the war. Back in Winston-Salem, instead of going to work in one of his family's banking and industrial organizations, he became a reporter, copy editor, feature writer, and columnist for the *Twin City Sentinel.* In his Sunday column "Out of Old Fields," a bit of poetry began to make its appearance, and a character for his first book was introduced. In 1949 he gave up the newspaper in order to devote his entire time to writing, though he had not always been able to do so. He has found that business, agricultural, and civic interests are quite demanding. He is married to the former Barbara Mildred Lasater, and they have three children.

Frank Borden Hanes is a meticulous writer. Still unpublished is his first effort, a novel in verse. Though he was not satisfied with it, he determined to use the form and technique a second time. The result was *Abel Anders* (1951), book-length narrative poem which won the Roanoke-Chowan Award. "There is a great place in our literature for narrative poetry," Hanes once said, "for you can say things in verse that you cannot say in prose," meaning that for him, at least, poetry permits a freedom otherwise impossible. *Abel Anders,* alternating lyric passages with poetic narrative, tells the story of a North Carolina mountain man who, seeking success and happiness, finds that though he can exploit others' weaknesses, he cannot solve the problem of self.

The Bat Brothers (1953) is a series of three psychological verse narratives, set in Montana of the 1870's. *The Fleet Rabble* (1961), prose novel about the Nez Percé Indians, won the Sir Walter Raleigh Award. There are many uncollected poems.

IN LABYRINTHS

In labyrinths are formed the isolations,
The hive within, the croft, the walls that bind;

So rise the hills whose shadows graze adjacent,
While on the plains grow fences of the mind.

THE PLAIN MAN

    The plain man stood before his car
With his son beside him,
And the shadow of dusk hung heavy
On the mountain chain and on the valley
Which bedded in the opaque mist of night.
As they stood, the moon
Passed above the horizon
And swung into the heavens,
And a black cloud hit her shoulder-high,
Hanging her with raven down
Like a large,
Oval-headed,
And motionless bird.

The man's son
Sat and said:

Where does peace come from, Father?
Where does the contentment
Of the moon come from?
And why is it the great searchlights
Pour out of the sky
Through the cloud slits
Like groping tentacles of silver?

The man cleared his throat
And pursed his bloodless lips.

Moonlight is but sunlight
In refraction, he said.
It is like shining a lantern
Into a mirror. . . .

OLD ARROWHEAD THOUGHTS OF A LATE WAR

Soon
now it
will be done
like strains maroon
shifting from teeth that grit
at death to a hopped-up sax's run
All over but one good rumble for the throng
all done but the idiotic righting of the wrong

May
will come
a tiptoe virgin
doe-eyed from delay
molested by drums of Harlem
Let silent buddies lie beyond urging
Don't we who pick a memory's tattered thread
make crowsfeet of the spool that binds us to the dead?

AU BEAU MILIEU

I read it in the Gita
Heard the Zendavesta's hue;
I learned it from Mohammed
And the Talmud of the Jew;

It runs through Buddhist scriptures
And the Bible's parallel:
The good all laugh in heaven
And the sinners screech in hell.

But if the Chinvad Bridge hurls
The wicked off in hate
And the saints greet their confessors
Inside the Pearly Gate,

What middle path is offered
To the billions morphodite
Who die and hang there spinning
In the silence-swarming night?

Or, look at it like this:
With both hell and heaven seen,
Just what's supposed to happen
To the neutrals inbetween?

POETRY REVIVAL

Old man, write your poem. I tell you this, your son,
gold-headed with a bit of tarnish in my short hair.
Write your poem for some hieroglyphics specialist among the
    bees.
Write it, for it lets you weep a little bit, to mourn
in print, whereas it is disgraceful for men to cry aloud.

What do you descry among the black images worthy of song?
What do you know of death as the very young know it,
who watch ants tote off great dessicated beetles,
doomed to an almost prenatal consciousness like salmon
who fight to high waters as sperm towards the womb?

What blind truth can you picture comparable
to the unnaturalness of life the child sees
in the laughable aquarium where fish feed on wounds?

What is it, old man, you write about worth writing?
What else is there to say when machines atomize flesh
like Vicks Vaporub? That it is bad? That death is sin?
While you count the slim lists of a dozen species
hounded to extinction since you first breathed air?

What crabs you old men are! you sick-fingered punchers
    of keys!

Of course we die! What else? The children read through ice.
Look at their cool faces turned to you.
It's too late to hunt the lion, for he's done in.
What prey remains?

Write your poem, old man. It's as good a way as any
to dole out the rhythms of the clock.

LOVE IS A BULLET

(*to P.R.*)

Green-yellow is the light,
Hanging like painted moss.
It breeds algae in the air.

I told a friend it would be thus.
I told him the azaleas had cold faces.
It was the time birds romped,
              deaf in laughter,
As the wind twisted them
              like nimble leaves,
Precursors to the months of peace.

I told this man that spring would come
And if he stopped a while with me
The faces of azaleas would turn around
              for him.

The birds would lose an acrobatic madness
And settle to the trees and sing, I swore.
They renew lost testaments of love
And raise old houses for the poor, I told him.

"But love is in a quarter inch of lead," he said.
"I know a cylinder it contains.
And, as for houses, there were none built
              to my dimensions.

I never owned a house or thought I should.
But still I keep one lover in reserve.
          Do you?

"He lies in the low magnitudes,
Closeted with Isolde
And the garments of Tristram.
There are no dust cloths in his house,
And that is one prerequisite of mine.
He does not burn an incense to the seasons,
And that would seem to be another.
His friends sit in symmetrical content
At conference with the skull of Kierkegaard.

"I think that now I'm ready to go home.
And, after all, what's in the song of birds
But only hymns to Him?"

He would not pause to listen.
And now it has come about much as I said,
And the air is green and quieter than grasses are
And the birds dip at azaleas, face to face,
Remembering there is a chore in blooming.

But he did not wait to see.
(He hated suns and used to pull the shade.)
And now the wind has sunk into the fluting
          veins of earth,
Throbbing down those undiscoverable tunnels
Which lead into that lover's domicile.

And he makes belated answer to the flutes
On the naked viol his breastbone is.

ELEANOR ROSS TAYLOR

WHEN RANDALL JARRELL was presented the National Book Award in 1961, he unexpectedly launched forth during the ceremonies into high praise of *Wilderness of Ladies,* saying he regretted that Eleanor Ross Taylor's book had not been the winner instead of his own *The Woman at the Washington Zoo.* He assured his great television audience "that in heaven or hell or wherever it is that good poets go, Hardy and Emily Dickinson are saying to all the new arrivals: 'Did you really see Eleanor Taylor?' . . . ." As a matter of record, *Wilderness of Ladies* had been enthusiastically received by reviewers and had sported a glowing introduction by Jarrell himself.

Eleanor Ross, born at Norwood (Stanly County), June 30, 1920, is sister of James Ross (author of the novel *They Don't Dance Much*) and Fred Ross (author of the novel *Jackson Mahaffey*) and Jean Ross (also a writer and wife of poet Don Justice). At the Woman's College of the University of North Carolina, she was active in literary groups and wrote for the campus publications. After teaching for two years, she went to Vanderbilt University for graduate study in English. She was married to the novelist and short story writer Peter Taylor in 1943. When he returned from war service in England, he accepted a professorship at the Woman's College, and they lived in Greensboro for several years. From 1949 to 1952 their base was Hillsboro, where they owned a beautiful old home. Mrs. Taylor continued to write poetry during the time her husband served on the faculties of the University of Chicago, Kenyon College, and the Ohio State University, his recent assignment. There have been frequent visits to and sojourns in Italy, France, and England. The Taylors have a daughter and a son.

Wilderness of Ladies (1960) is composed of twenty-eight poems—deft, strange, unique. The people in them—can anyone doubt they derive from the Yadkin River valley of piedmont North Carolina?—are gentle folk. "The poems and poet come out of the Puritan South," wrote Randall Jarrell. "This Scotch Presbyterianism translated into the wilderness is, for her, only the fierce shell of its old self, but it is as forbidding and compulsive as ever: the spirit still makes its unforgiving demands on a flesh that is already too weak to have much chance in the struggle."

SONG

Oh my dearie,
Our childhoods are histories,
Buckets at the bottom of the well,
And hard to tell
Whether they will hold water or no.
Did Pa die before we were married?
No, he died in twenty-seven,
But I remember the wedding
Reminded me of the funeral—
When the grandbabies ask,
Little do they care,
I will tell them about the man I found
That day at my plowing in the low-grounds
Lying at the edge of the water.
His face had bathed five nights.
A dark man, a foreigner, like.
They never found his kin to tell. . . .
Buckets, buckets at the bottom of the well.
It was in the paper with my name.
I found him.
I have the clipping tells all about it,
If your Grandma aint thrown it out.

Oh my dearie
When our faces are swol up
We will look strange to them.
Nobody, looking out the door
Will think to call us in.
They'll snap their fingers trying
To recollect our names.
Five nights, five bones, five buckets—
Who'll ever hear a sound?
Oh my dearie
The rope broke
The bucket bobs round
Oh my dearie

BUCK DUKE AND MAMMA

He came bringing us a milkpail full
Of speckled, wild, goose plums—
All fat unsmelt-out perfumedom—
And perched on the back porch curb to taste a few.
"Sour! Your eyes'll water, Miss Tempe!
But sweet, too."
Mamma's way was posing by the silent pool
And tossing in the line amiss
That shook the skies of the other world
And all but loosed the roots of this.
She trimmed and trained the roundabout backwoods,
Was glad that Buck Duke had a devilish eye;
It saved an orphan from dire fortitude,
And saved his grandpa's house from sanctity.
"Your Papa doesn't favor your going there.
I say, enter evil to cure evil, if you dare!"
As she went about her cast-off household chores
She overlooked them with a lavish bow
Inspired by that heroine of poems,
Her elocution teacher, Miss Hattie Yow.
    "Nothing to do? In this world of ours?
      Where weeds spring daily amidst sweet flowers?"
    Your-mammy-never-came-to-much-my-Buck.

"Don't drink that Mackling Spring's brack water
Whe'r it's high or low.
The cows stand in there and let go."
But old Duke's beardy words were moss for campfire
When they took their kitchen rations to the woods.
Mamma's boys looked out for sassafras, but Buck
Made frog gigs, thrashed Mackling Spring into a suds.
("I say, dear boys! Be good. Take care.
But learn a little evil! if you dare....")
His thirst once drunk, turned drunken,
And Buck Duke tossed all night, all day,
Made rusty speeches on old swapping knives,

Called names that paled the sallow-boned herbwives,
Tore off the sleeping clothes, his bed's, his own,
And never seemed to wake.
His boyish modesty ran dry,
At last the hands cooled, then the face.
Mamma stood at his bedside.
She overlooked him with a sprightly brow
Inspired by that gay mistress of mad poesy
Her elocution teacher, Miss Hattie Yow.
    " 'Stop stop pretty waters' cried Mary one day
      'My vessel, my flowers you carry away.' "

Mamma made a wreath of all her flowers:
The histrionic garden did not bear
One saucy pose when she put down the scissors;
The battered bees hung stupid in mid-air.
She worked on knees and elbows on the back porch,
That savage zinnia ornament compiled,
Then all at once cooped up her face
With hands like bird's wings—
A gesture, she knew, would have made Miss Hattie
    smile.

IN THE CHURCHYARD

In the churchyard I hear them hammering
On the new roof of my new house
A hundred years old.
Cupped acorns glut the walks,
The greenish nuts crushed in.
Cupped earths hold up the bright memorial ferns.
They're gone!
Down over Mamma's face
They nailed, we nailed, I nailed the lid.
And there was Uncle Risdon.
Married a Miss Catherine Tye. Aunt Catherine
Somehow I can't now call her full name.
She took a galloping consumption

After she let the baby catch on fire.
Aunt Oratha despised the coat
That Uncle bought her. She died of pride.
Pride knoweth neither hot nor cold
But hers knew both.
They die of fleshly pride.
And Cousin Mazeppa took laudanum.
"Why did you do it, Zeppie, girl?
Wa'n't Daddy good to you?"
"Pray, let me sleep!"

Child, brave it to blind-out the fur
Of the evergreens in sun above:
They are too far;
Shade has rinsed out their sun,
Hushed up their green.
They'll dizzy one.

There's the rattat of the hammers—
The little nails, the little nails,
The birds eat out one's hands!

MADAME

This is the sleep that fell just after dinner.

These are the windows that let in the sleep
That fell just after dinner.

This is the light that shed through the windows
That let in the sleep that fell just after dinner.

These are the lids that shut out the light
That shed through the windows
That let in the sleep that fell just after dinner.

These are the kisses the size of quarters that lay
On the lids that shut out the light that shed

Through the windows that let in the sleep
That fell just after dinner....

Let us put them on her tray for a tip....

Oh, thank you, Madame!
It was like you, to make life pleasant
Somehow,
Living or sleeping.

UNCLE

(from "Family Bible")

Typical of the presents
Grandma gave Grandpa
Was Uncle Mun,
A baroque buckle
Not to be undone.
He thought before he spoke,
Abstained from drink, snuff, smoke,
Marriage; ate and dressed frugally,
Reproved respectfully
His mother's yen
For jet beads on her birthday.
Was it not thoughtful of him
On her busy death day
As she counted quilt-blocks
To elicit this data
In Spencerian pencil
Laid away in the clock
For me,
Posterity?
    My full name is Aminta Dunlap Watkins Ross.
    My mother was Merina Wilkerson.
    My father was Arnold Watkins—he carpentered—
    I married your pa Whitson Ross
    My wedding presents were a feather bed and two hens.

GRANDDAUGHTER

(from "Family Bible")

When she was old, deaf, widowed, my grandmother,
She came to spend a lonely night at home.
When I went to call her in to breakfast
She did not hear my brave voice for her comb
Running through her hair in little flights—
(Long, long hair as much gold as white,
Flying with old-fashioned electricity
From the comb's old-fashioned friction)
And as she rocked, her shell-combs on her knee.
Suddenly aware, she looked up at me
Through her shimmering hair, startled, and smiled.
Air ye awake, little gal?
Perhaps she thought I was admiring her.
She gave a proud, delighted, sidewise smile
Flashing her small gray teeth and elf-arched eyes,
For a ninety-eight-point-six degrees' response.
But she was disappointed, though I smiled.
Her silent island threatened me enchantment;
The joints too lithe to creak when I bent over
Sailed off without retrieving for her
A big bone hairpin wrecked upon the floor.

The day she was buried
I played sick and lay abed
Claiming fever.
I did not see her dead.
But eight months before
At Rehobath Church
On Homecoming Day
I stood with a crowd
Of boys and girls, and
Watched her cross the churchyard
Slowly, alone; from end to end
She crossed the yard,

Her head thrown back,
Swathed deep in black—
Long skirts, pointed black toes,
The wind parting her many veils,
The blue eyes beneath roving, veiled—
And leaning on a stick.
She seemed a giant Figure,
All eyes upon her;
Yet none spoke.
And all my heart said,
Run to her! Claim her!
(Wild loneliness that
Beats its wings on death)
Then the spell broke.
We who had waved across so many chasms
No longer had to say we were not close.
Was closeness more than painful separateness?
We were a constellation of detached, like, ghosts.

WILL INMAN

THE INTENT of Will Inman as a poet has been to explore the greatness of man, who has "multitudes" within him which rarely find expression; always man must keep in mind what a tremendous capacity he has to realize himself and to respond to others. Will Inman—whose literary cousins are Emerson and Whitman, Dylan Thomas, Hart Crane and Thomas Wolfe—has examined himself and his environs in four publications of poetry: *Lament and Psalm* (1960), *I Am the Snakehandler* (1960), *A River of Laughter* (1961), and *Honey in the Blood* (1962).

Will Inman is the pen name of William A. McGirt, Jr., born in Wilmington, May 4, 1923. After local schooling he went to Duke University, from which he graduated in 1943. After serving as a time-study man in a shipyard and working at the University Library at Chapel Hill, he was engaged for nine years (1947-56) in left-wing activity for labor unions and the Progressive Party. At first he was struck "by the emptiness and barrenness of much of our life in this period," he says, but afterwards he discovered that the "mere imposition of any social system from 'without' will not heal a sick people, that learning and healing can come only to those who genuinely want it and then, in inspiration, by mutual creative example, from the awakening of inner capacities." For six years he worked in meat and fish markets, having been blackballed for better jobs as a result of his political radicalism. In 1956 he went to New York and worked at the Yale Club Library. His poetry, written since the age of seven, at this point ceased to be propagandistic. Later, following some months in a mail-order house, he became connected with the library at New York University, where he has held numerous positions.

Though he has written short stories, novels, and essays, Will Inman considers himself primarily a poet. His poetry activities consume several active hours every day, much of his work "aimed at intervolving the inner and outer landscapes." Though his mother's maiden name was actually Inman, the pseudonym is more an expression of "the will-in-man that is not mere will-power but moves with nerve-identity with the creative center, the Laughter of Affirmative Real." Will Inman says he craves no wide audience, just a few responding readers.

WHERE WILLOW IS A LIMBER SWITCH

Where willow is a limber switch I bend to drink . . and,
   when I lift my head, is a tree bent over me
   yellow budful, and green lacings hang
   around my shoulders and lean in my eyes.

Still the sun in rounds thru slanteye leaves is
   the sound of water rocking its low swells
   up thru my thirst, till I sing low and hush
   swift full of listening and a quiet burst
   of glad O to my fingersfro.

And I drink again while the tree drinks of the creek
   and of sun and of me, yes, and graps the quag
   and graps the yonder and heaves a silence
   and hangs again down now I drink the naked
   sun thru the whippers.

Where willow is an old stump I bend to drink . . and,
   when I lift my head, is a blue limb bent over me
   yellow budful, and a green wind soughs down
   around my shoulders and strings my eyes
   with salt dew . . till a limber switch
   is a last last laugh up a bent limb blue.

LYRIC

    A thrush of wind sang thru the air
    and broke the crystal silence where
    the nest of twilight gave to night
    old songs of broken-crystal light.

    A thrush of blood sings thru my veins
    and wakes the love long silence wanes
    with waiting. O the nest of dawn
    consumes old songs to nourish one!

TREE WILL MOW THICKETS

hHahh!
Hew the main stem (hHahh!) Tree will mow thickets when it
 falls (hHahh!). Here in the greygreen shadows (hHahh!)
 sunsplayed thru tall vined trees (hHahh!) gray-black-
 and-white swallowtail burtles swift (hHahh!) with
 long wingtips white spiralling (hHahh!) trail of
 wonder in my (hHahh!) eyes.

Axeblade sings (hHahh!) on widening white. Sweat (hHahh!)
 dews on forehead (hHahh!). Eyes go relentless to the
 (hHahh!) wound. Great tree trembles. (hHahh!)
 One more (hHahh!) .. just one more (hHahh!) ...
 T I M B E R ! — Get back, Boy!   Whooo - eeeeee!
 Crash!

Limbs flounce and fall back, wrong. Thickets mowed under.
 Zebra swallowtail effervesces out of dust and sprung
 dew, or in toward the dark untouched. Big naked blue
 wound thru roof of the woods. Yellow eye relentless
 to the wound. More steps in the brush, then

hHahh!

DILATION

So my songs hurt your ears, so the hard words hang up in the
 narrows of your hearing, so the meanings and the sounds
 jostle against confusion; so, in your hurt, you cry out
 and push me away.

But I do not move away. I lunge more fierce against you,
 my words find seminal anchor in your ear, beyond your
 hearing, deep in you where there is something of us
 inseparable and beyond even our now knowing, even beyond
 this lunge and jet and hurt and passion, beyond aggress,
 beyond submit, even beyond this lock-holt embrace.

For you must dilate to bear seed, you must expand to hold
   all I am, to be all you are. No, Man, don't you shrink
   away sweating and crimson, you too must dilate or wither
   sterile in the hearing and shouting. You also know
   already what I say, and you want Open Thru to your already
   knowing. Listen, listen and sing me back fierce songs!

Yes, even so, I. I dilate in your cry, in your hesitation,
   in your confusion and revulsion and outrage, even so
   do I dilate and receive your anger and grow. And then
   when you learn to love me, all that I am, all that you
   are in me, then I too were large enough, dilate enough,
   strong and wide in my embrace enough, to love you as you
   are you and as I am I and as we in our fury and wonder
   Are!

ON SEVEN HILLS

On seven hills the blue rapport
of distance drew us out of time,
yet never tore us root from limb
nor taught us to deny the earth.

We followed paths that reached for heights
where we became one being, knew
the hungry rhythms underneath
that thru us fed themselves the sky.

Our trails, though separate awhile,
shall ever join upon the hills
where thru our roots we drink the sky
and thru our limbs we feed the earth.

THE DISTANCE IN YOUR TOUCH

Your closeness is not near enough:
the distance in your touch compels
a reckoning of spacial stuff—
a face-to-facing of mere shells.

Then eye strikes eye—what swiftening chords
inspire the whole implicit score
of music tangent in the words
the heart intones thru eye-rapport!

If lips could take the radiant stroke,
transfer the light thru fluent pane
of blood, such awkward words we spoke
were not redundant nor in vain.

But lips are flesh .. and cannot tell
how limbs have crippled love—how words
or kisses lash the eyes, expel
thru wounds the tortured blood of chords.

A BLOWN NEWSPAPER

Sun lay down orange on a cloud,
wind prowled and blew where day was,
no moon rose, trees rocked and soughed,
and the dead street held expectant pause
in darkness and neon light,
but nothing happened. You recall
such times when eery thru the night
or day in time of storm when all
things stood tense and the world held
her own breath while the wind blew
its anger out . . . a few trees, felled . . .
and listening heartbeats hastened, grew.

A blown newspaper then has sense
of bitterness across the stone
like an autumn leaf falling, tense
no more . . . but lost, and lone, alone.
You've been alone when waiting hours
are turgid as harkening ears
and the pavement is alive with flowers
of love's returning feet . . . your tears
fall salt and bitter: would the rain
could wash so deep a bitterness,
the stone is grey, as grey as pain . . .
and the blown paper's emptiness . . . .

BE

I know I need not wait nor run to meet you, yet
you move athwart my parallel,
still in your own
compass . . . in a wake that crosses,
widens, mine.
Fins flash, wings splash.

So, out of a deep rocking wet,
I move fullward
upon where I am less if not all. And so,
our fathoms lock without fins—armless!
wingless! still move free, lock with perfect
nowness, now unlock and still move free
together.

Be my deep friend.

Be my deep.

Be!

GUY OWEN

That a poet's life is one of seclusion, an existence far from the push of contemporary living, is of course a romantic notion without much historical basis. Certainly Guy Owen would deny the separation of poet from commonplace activities. He worked on a farm and in a tobacco warehouse, was general handyman about a filling station, waited on tables at a restaurant, was welder in a shipyard, and did a stint with the Army in Europe. Though serious poetry came later, all this time it was being generated.

He was born on February 24, 1925, near Clarkton in Bladen County. Here in the Cape Fear River tobacco county, he grew up. His first printed poem was sent to a newspaper by his high school English teacher. By the time he entered the University of North Carolina in 1942, he was determined to follow a career of writing and teaching. After graduation in 1947, with time out for the Army service, he followed his bachelor's degree with a master's and a doctorate in Elizabethan literature at Chapel Hill. Meanwhile he had begun college teaching at Davidson and Elon, and for seven years was at Stetson University in Florida. In the fall of 1962 he returned home by joining the Department of English at N. C. State College, where his specialty is the teaching of creative writing.

Besides a number of short stories, he has written a novel, *Season of Fear* (1960), which was both a critical and popular success. It used a setting similar to the Bladen County of his birth. At Stetson he established *Impetus*, a poetry magazine first confined to student poetry but later opened to poets everywhere. *Southern Poetry Today* (1962) is a chapbook he co-edited to indicate the current trends of regional verse. *Cape Fear Country and Other Poems* (1958) is a collection of his own work, which has also appeared from time to time in *Poetry, Saturday Review, College English* and over two dozen other magazines, as well as several anthologies.

Guy Owen's role is that of observer, of perceiver. Though some of his inspiration comes from the classroom, he is more often drawn to the Carolina low country and to the mountains, where near Moravian Falls he spends the summers with his wife Dorothy and their two sons.

IT IS NOT THE SEA

It is not the sea that drowns us;
We drown who only guess at gulls.

It is the daily dust, insidious
And fine, that sifts the rancid air;
It is the subtle mote that seeps through walls
And floods our chartered rooms,
The risky film upon the tide
Of quiet streets, unseen, but there.
This bloats the rotting lung,
This seals tired eyelids down
And mutes the blunted tongue.
It is the daily dust that silts the nostrils up
And clots the singing blood:

It is not by sea we drown.

THE WHITE STALLION

A white horse came to our house once
Leaping like dawn the backyard fence.
In dreams I heard his shadow fall
Across my bed. A miracle,
I woke beneath his mane's surprise;
I saw my face within his eyes,
The dew ran down his nose and fell
Upon the bleeding window quince....

But long before I broke the spell
My father's curses sped him on,
Four flashing hooves that bruised the lawn.
And as I stumbled into dawn
I saw him scorn a final hedge,
I heard his pride upon the bridge;
Then through the wakened yard I went
To read the rage the stallion spent.

THE SOLITARY HORSEMAN

"Parents are advised against giving a child a rocking horse because it does not develop the group spirit."

I'll buy a horse for my young son
And help him on it. Whereupon
I pray he'll spur across the floor
And, solitary, leap the door

And paltry shrub. I'll hear one hoof,
Arrogant against the roof:
Then all below will see and cry,
"What bold rider usurps the sky!"

OLD HUNTER

The heart was ever a hunting thing
   But the bones of men rebel,
And I'll rise no more to the whirring wing
   Though the season's good for quail.

Though the moon lies cold on sedge and briar
   I'll draw my chair to the hearth;
Though the fox cries out to the moon on fire
   My Buck keeps still in the earth.

Hunters I knew lie down in the broom
   Where the black bat trails his wing,
And what they scent in the narrow room
   I weep for remembering. . . .

The Hound I'll hunt has a giant foot
   And a hungry star in his eye.
The hulking Bear I aim to shoot
   Will bleed through the burning sky.

AUNT ELLA

Dear Aunt Ella, who warred with dirt,
Is laid beneath the dust, inert.
And now we pause and bring to mind
How all her pots and windows shined;

How forth she marched with deadly rag,
A brush her sword, a mop her flag,
To drive some mote beyond her door
That dared profane her sacred floor.

But now though dirt beleagues her room
Aunt Ella never lifts a broom:
If you would keep her, Lord, you must
Give her a mansion rife with dust.

HAWK

Brute hawk wings pump the livid air
And spell my yard. His shadow slants,
A hungry curse that bruises light
And chills the blood beneath his shank.

Nothing not stone could bear desire
So strong in eye or wing. The urge
To life recalls too late the chick
Where shadow and source converge. . . .

Mine the cry your talons tear,
Mine the down, your noon-day haul;
And my hunger hovers where
Spills the blood our beak lets fall.

OLD TOBEY

Old Tobey had a way of judging man,
Not by deeds, by what he shaped by hand.
He claimed no man could hide behind his work—
No weakness safe from eye, no hidden quirk
But left some sign to him. The farmer's flaw
He guessed by stands of corn or rye he saw,
Driving his wagon by. Half-empty bins
Revealed to him the owner's sins,
The subtle sins beneath the stunted bean.
"No crooked man can lay a furrow clean,"
He said, "nor ever bring full harvest in."
And so he spoke of other trades and men.
And though old Tobey lived and judged us long,
I never met the man who proved him wrong.

THE CONSPIRACY

Here where deer cross over at dark
The pavement gives; it bears the mark
Of hunted hooves that scrape and thin
The road where snorting bucks plunge in,

And there, there sedge has leaped the fence;
It wears the mask of innocence
And, silent, gnaws the yielding tar,
Hiding the place where tunnels are

Mined by rain. Even ants conspire
To haul cement along the briar
And live oaks thrust a levered root
That cracks the surface, foot by foot.

I should report this subtle crime,
And oh I shall, but in due time:
Let it be in another season
When I've lost all heart for treason.

DESERTED FARM

I took a walk through woods and snow
Until I came to a garden row
Claimed by sedge, then a gate of boards
Rotting beneath three martin gourds.

A roofless shed, an old turn plow
Said men were here, but not here now.
"Where have they gone?" I asked the pump
Rusting beside a lightwood stump.

Its handle swept toward the sky
(Whatever that might signify);
Its mouth was dry as chimney clay—
And if it knew, it didn't say.

SPLIT-RAIL FENCE

The way a split-rail fence has failed
To hold its beauty back, old rails
Too tired, too gnarled and weather-maimed,
Itself too random to contain
Wild blooms that spill between and over
(Queen Anne's lace, blue grass, and clover)
That somersault down the mountain slope,
Like water from the mountain spring,
Has stirred in me some secret hope
Not born of the buoyant spring,
Has cheered me over a road accurst
And slaked a deeper thirst.

ROBERT WATSON

Though Robert Watson happens to be a professor of English, he does not think that his day-to-day duties on campus have anything particularly to do with his being a poet. A poet may be anyone curious about what is inside people. "Poetry hits at our private lives," he once said. It is about "hate, joy, lust, fear, love, despair—the feelings we try to hold down in society. . . . It tries to come to terms with what we find hard to reconcile ourselves to: unfulfilled desire, old age, death. . . ."

He was born December 26, 1925, in Passaic, New Jersey, where he grew up and began writing poems in high school. At Williams College, from which he graduated in 1946, he continued to write. When it became clear that teaching was to be his profession, he went to Johns Hopkins University for a master's degree, then followed it with a Ph.D. there in 1955. By that time, he had been an instructor in English in both institutions and had come, in 1953, to the Woman's College of the University of North Carolina, where he is now associate professor. He was attracted to Greensboro because he found there a heartening balance between the scholarly and the creative in English studies. For a year he was in Europe as a Swiss-American exchange fellow at the University of Zurich, and in 1961 spent a season in New York on a Research League fellowship. He is married to the artist Elizabeth Rean, and has a son and daughter. Besides the English novel and modern literature, on which he concentrates in the classroom, his special interest is the work of George Meredith, on whom he has written a number of articles. In 1962, reassured by success in a poetry contest sponsored by the *American Scholar*, he brought out a distinguished first collection, *A Paper Horse*.

Critics have been hard-pressed to place Watson in any school of poetry. Perhaps his own words will provide a hint: "I like to think of them [his poems] as I think of the old ballads, fairy tales, history, drama; narrative verse. . . . These poems are intended to give what poetry can give a man: pleasure, consolation." His grotesques, which blend into the familiar, are compacted of an almost surrealistic invention heightened by a sly, joyous verbal wit.

FIRST MAN ON VENUS

She stood for love:
Thighs, lids heavy, milk heavy,
Made for the White City
We all seek.

To have had her then!
Her body swollen, all sour now.
To have had her then!

Venus was cloudy.
I did not see the White City.
I saw nothing. Was nothing there?
I was the first man, the first man
To visit Venus
And return.

HALLOWEEN: A POEM FOR CHILDREN

Old orange hollow head, eyes aflame,
    Brains in the garbage pail,
With senseless grin now welcome
    The ghosts to the door.
Where you happier curled asleep,
    Sucking the sun's color,
    Dandled by Autumn?

See the ghosts—small hands reaching out
    For the bell, wailing "Trick or Treat,"
And pennies, candy and fruit
    Slide under the giggling sheet.
You are a man for a night;
    They are what frightens them.

WINTER LOVERS

Hesitant we stand by a sled at the top of the hill
Our eyes measuring down white lamp and star lit road,
Down beyond the road's end to the back of black woods,
Then up to an equally black sky, yet interspersed with stars.
Here the white is gathered and up there dispersed.
Stopped measuring, our eyes swerve to each other,
And we each see circular black with white around.

I pull our sled some steps more up, then running throw
It on the ice, myself on top, and she in its sliding past
Flings herself on my back, arms around my neck.
And so on runners over ice and snow we lovers
Of simple black and white hurtle through our nights,
Avoiding black, holding to white; we never look to left or
    right.

MOST WANTED

You smile a plump uncle smile,
A Christmas smile around your pipe,
Smile down from the wall, the Post Office wall.
Your greying hair, your smile says . . .
But words over you say, "WANTED BY THE FBI
For Double Murder, Arson."
(Your own wife, your own one-year-old child)
We can't read on.

You look the same; the child we knew
Smiles through the man we listened to,
Who held us by our ears, a bore,
(A bum, your father said) a sculptor,
Lover of Thoreau.

". . . to see differently,
To be free to see,
To throw off clocks, scales, yardsticks,

To find truth under all this absurdity . . ."
You smiled forgiveness on such fools as we,
Especially when your beer was free.
What was it you could, we couldn't see, didn't know?
You wore sandles, we wore shoes.
You said you'd hammer life from stone
Into . . . What? We never knew;
You did not put your bronze and stone on view;
Certainly you beat and blew about our ears
A Walden we were not admitted to.

Most wanted now
Your fame hangs in every town.
At last you made your neighbors see
Life's uncorked absurdity,
Escaped into a world where
Clocks, scales, yardsticks
Are thrown down.
You hammered life from flesh, from bone,
And fired what housed the foolish life,
Your child, your wife.
Your work is done.
You smile in peace at us, the absurd.
You made your word flesh,
Flew from our state and now pursued,
Your face in every gallery, every town
Smiles its Christmas smile down.
Most wanted, you don't want us.

ON STAGE, OFF STAGE

I've buried Troy, I've conquered Rome
And Hollywood. My crown, my head
Roll in a trunk with other parts
I wear. This is the good Lord's beard
I wore the day I made Adam,
Adam's fig leaf when I was he,
My horns for Mephistopheles . . .
Hamlet, Vanya, Lear, and Faust
Lie here. I shut the coffin's lid.
Curtain down, clothes, lives removed
I search the program for my name
In vain. What was it? I don't know.
Another life, name so long ago.

Find the birthmark on my elbow,
Tell me the nurse's error,
Of a changeling. "You are, you are . . .
The eldest son, the only heir . . ."
Curtain before he tells my name.

No more of men, no more of gods,
The dreams of men, the dreams of gods.
No more of parts, of parts of parts
Made up by men who made up life.
I'll play spaces between stars,
Dust rising from dancer's feet.
The world sprouts from my trunk, my limbs.
My leaves, our stars, whisper: "You have
No name."
        I am now satisfied.

O. B. HARDISON, JR.

THAT POETRY CAN BE a proper adjunct of reading, teaching, and study is well illustrated by the work of Osborne Bennett Hardison, Jr. If his poems sometimes seem difficult, this is probably due to the reader's lack of acquaintance with their literary background. Yet this is not always true, and any reader with or without academic equipment will delight in such selections as "Primitivism."

O. B. Hardison, Jr., was born October 22, 1928, in San Diego, California, where his father, member of a Wadesboro family, was stationed as a Naval officer. After a youth spent moving from west coast to east coast and back again, he concluded his preparatory training at St. Albans School in Washington, D. C. By this time, he was writing poetry regularly. One year at the Massachusetts Institute of Technology studying physical chemistry was enough for a young man hungering for the humanities, and he transferred to the University of North Carolina. There, because of overcrowded living conditions, he lived in a tent behind the law building, only a stone's throw from his classes in English. He helped edit *Factotum*, a literary magazine. In Dr. J. O. Bailey's course in Victorian literature, he met Marifrances Fitzgibbon, and they were married. With bachelor's and master's degrees, he set out for the University of Wisconsin, from which he was awarded the Ph.D. in 1956. Meanwhile, he went as a Fulbright Fellow to Rome, where, he says, he "wrote poetry, sampled Italian wines, and worked at times on a dissertation concerning Renaissance literary criticism." Following instructorships in English at the University of Tennessee and at Princeton, he returned in 1957 to Chapel Hill. He has six children, four girls and two boys.

His *Lyrics and Elegies* was published in Scribner's *Poets of Today V* (1958). In an Introduction, John Hall Wheelock observed that Hardison's delight is with the music of ideas. "The subject matter of poetry," says Hardison, "is not man or actions or nature but always and inevitably is *value*"—value to the extent of truth as any poet can discover it. Often there is humor, and always there is a total craftsmanship. Other books of his are *Modern Continental Literary Criticism* (1962) and *The Enduring Monument* (1962).

OF MOTION

Ambition is the young man's sinecure.
You know that life is motion to the last.
Your wealth will all go begging to the poor.
Your sailors will not cut you from the mast.

Beneath the lunar sphere all lines are straight
And you must turn and turn and turn again.
Catastrophes come knocking at the gate
And you must turn the key and let them in.

Your glassy girl in never what she seems.
Her body withers on the seamy bed.
Her floor is built on crooked enthymemes.
Her roof is turning over overhead.

God is a circle radiating birth.
You are refracted from the glistening flood.
Fertility is burning up the earth.
(I contemplate the Beautiful and Good.)

I said the dead have learned to cease to move.
Green conflagrations devastate the bride.
You are an ember in the emerald stove
And I, said Aristotle, and he cried.

PRIMITIVISM

Would God that I might be an ape
And shuffle off this human shape.
From pressing cares and discord free
I'd dangle from a mango tree;
My eyes would glitter and my nose
Would nudge the dirt between my toes.
My bulging head and tiny brain
Would give me then no cause for pain;
My mangy fur would be a house
In winter for the grazing louse.
And in my bulging navel I
Would contemplate infinity.

THE ST. PETERSBURG PARADOX

If you agree, agree to be indifferent.
The soul's exchange is strict: great speculators
May gain a world but mostly lose their shirts.

The talent that is death to hide is death
To risk upon the spinning of a wheel
And lose, and we are not elect and lose.

Luck is a dream. The odds are on the house.
Not lovers but accountants supervise
The black and crimson tables of the heart.

So kiss me and keep your love. Instead of light
We'll take the darkness and endure our passion
Nailed hand and foot to one another's fear.

Turn out the light, and then turn out the light.
We'll ease our pain, and when the day arrives,
Put on our emptiness and try to sleep.

GIRL WITH GUITAR
To S. G.

See on those six high wires how her fingers
In a flickering dance (though random to my dazzled
Eye) defy the deep, and balancing on touch
Imponderable, measure the trembling lines,
Gamut from grumbling bass to glittering treble,
And strike the note of peril that we live.

And now involved in moving harmonies
Whose motions are the nations of the air
Whose time is pattern shifting in the light,
The heart grown reckless from those airs of grace
And tunes of glory, vibrates on its pegs,
And she, all glitter in the golden fields,
Alone and splendid, is its only song.

IMPRESSIONS

The cool and violent night
Somewhere arranges
Around corners
The parts of its dream.

The cool and violent night
Ridges the dark places
Strange with the fume of dreams
And yellow lights
(There is always a darkness).

The night is a time
In the yellow light to admire loss.
There are lights in the sky (there are places)
And yellow lights (and names)
And all this is moving
And the good ground almost imperceptibly
As though breathing moving
As though the roads and channels of all the air were moving
And we were part of them
And the lights moving in a great pinwheel like the sound
    of love
(For we are always part of them
Being moved by love and the admiration of loss).

Day of fire
Driving through the heart
(Being lost within love)
Ourselves (the violence).

TO FORD, GUGGENHEIM, ROCKEFELLER, ETC.

Reader of this poetry, stay.
I offer you undying fame,
And immortality of name,
But in return, you have to pay.

Virgil praised Caesar's feet of clay,
And Ovid praised his daughter's charm,
And Horace got his Sabine farm,
But rich Maecenas had to pay.

A mistress lives through Du Bellay,
While Spenser sang the Virgin Queen;
John Donne was witty but obscene,
But always, someone had to pay.

Rimbaud was just a little gay,
Maurice still more, Marcel the most,
But each knew how to tell a host
His duty to the Muse was—pay.

So rent me a house on Naples' bay
Where I can feel the tears of things
And think what song the siren sings
And how to make you, patron, pay.

MIDDLE PASSAGE

If Lazarus (says the great Pascal)
Dreams every night beneath the rain
He is the richest of them all,

While Dives surfeited in vain
Begs for a nightly crust of bread
Across the deserts of his brain,

Who is the loser; who's ahead?

Life is a toss—for every tail
You get a head with eyes to cry
And tongue to curse its last betrayal;

And every curse becomes a sigh
On lips grown passionate with tears,
And without words, there is no lie,
And if the cock crows, no one cares.

SPECULATIONS

Across the void's indifferent flood
The atoms drift like lazy snow;
In metaphysical cold blood
They'll kill the mind that thought them so.

Not warmth or light or subtle *I*
That's crucified on its own stick,
Or soundness or infirmity
Exist within the *Ding an sich*.

Outside titanic powers rave
And batter at our puny walls;
Let us be thankful for our cave
And whistle till the ceiling falls.

Yet I would gladly leave my home
For some remote and flowering south
And crush like honey from the comb
The naked sweetness of your mouth.

JONATHAN WILLIAMS

Born March 8, 1929, in Asheville, Jonathan Williams assists in the operation of an apple orchard at his home near Highlands when not engaged in one of his several professional roles: book designer, lecturer, publisher, and poet. Highlands is home base from which he ranges to display his Jargon Press publications and read his poems at college campuses and in coffee houses, perhaps in San Francisco, maybe in New York, often in Europe, anywhere.

After two years at Princeton, he attended the Institute of Art in Chicago, then completed his education at Black Mountain College in western North Carolina. There he became interested in the "new" poetry and contributed to the *Black Mountain Review*. Later, with the Army Medical Corps in Stuttgart, he worked with German printers and evolved an aesthetic of graphic arts. From his Jargon Press, initiated in 1951, have come more than fifty books by such writers as Kenneth Patchen, Charles Olson, Denise Levertov, Robert Creeley, Kenneth Rexroth, and Henry Miller, as well as publications of his own. Williams, who held a Guggenheim Fellowship in 1957, says that baseball and jazz are his two non-literary enthusiasms.

Broadsides and book titles are *Garbage Litters the Iron Face of the Sun's Child* (1951), *Red/Gray* (1952), *Four Stoppages* (1953), *The Empire Finals at Verona* (1959), *Amen/Huzza/Selah* (1960), and *In England's Green &* (1962). He is by no means a Beat Poet, though he has been connected with the movement and has been included in several anthologies: *The Beat Scene: The New American Poetry, 1945-1960;* and *'Beat Poets'* published in London.

No orthodox approach will serve the reader in *understanding* his poems: for instance, his lines cannot be paraphrased. Rhythm takes the place of paraphrasable meaning. It is the "noise" (Williams' word) within the lines the reader must hear—the pulsing jazz meters. One chosen word, as though sounded by an instrument, suggests another, and so on to the end of the poem. This method is of course a reaction to tradition and formality. While anti-intellectual in the academic sense, his poems uphold liberation and free expression, while decrying post-war pretense and gloom.

3 SIT-INS AGIN . . .

1. *S. O'Hara Digs Histry*

   couth
   Sooth

   (befo de Wa)

   no
   Ocacay
   Olacay!

   onay itshay?
   Ofay
   Lady

2. *The Interstate Pomegranate* (for Igal Roodenko and Bayard Rustin, Class of 1947)

   Kora
   in Hell;
   C. O. R. E.
   in Chapel
   Hill

   the Lady takes a back seat
   for six months;

   my friends refused a back seat,
   got thirty days once

3. *The Patagonian Declaration of Independence*

   o

   foot that can't be Beat
   carry me back
   to the Big-Foot Country,
   to the cool-yclept
   Coltrane Country

go

catch a catarrhed eel
in the know, if he's
hollow let him

be

cause when ah die
there'll be a Tah-Heel

bourne

THE ROUGH DAY

for Robert Creeley

Summer mounts
for war,
        climbing trees like a green idiot,

fires a salvo, a
blackbird barrage, dartingly, redwings
flashing 'O,

          they got me!' the bedazzled down the hall
uttered utterly . . .

His dirge, a clicking
of castanets
(the hi-fi

A tropical heat, a blood
orange

Everything, beckoning from Buncombe
County

A SPIN

I cut the stuff,
a whole blue field: figwort
's what they call it

This particular day I put a car thru it,
very fast,
out the gate, second gear, sharp right—

out of ourselves also say,
a few miles only, but

quite out, and up:
Highest Point East of South Dakota, it said—
6684,
oldest mountains on earth, etc.,
for what's in that

What good is a mountain without people? was all
he could ask

Sure, it's what I mean—
if not, to hell with it!
I can, he said, regain composures,
and not only there . . .

The sun, suddenly hot on my hands,
holding the steering wheel;
the shadow of two ravens quickly across the car,
a dead raccoon by the road . . .

There are other things, I said, besides, say, air,
which, ok, you have to breathe, ok,
so also you gotta eat—like light or space,
or a mountain, very much,

which, if you'd climb the highest, works
well

OUR DUSK: THAT WEST

once here
  my love
    where a sun hung caught
    in hemlock
    & fiery wind came
    washing up the creekbed
we lay
  my love
    on lichend rock, in pressures of
    the booming summertime
    at Scaly mountain
under lightning we lay
  my love
in vapor flashing, rains down once
    on water/sand
        (turnd in the current, alert)
      & loved
        til now:
            when sun, once here
            may strike,
            where ash is
            thick, where we got up
where also the lightning
struck thru the face,
& it is dry,
  my love

CREDO

    I do
dig Everything Swinging (thinking

as I do:

ah, art
is fro-

zen Zen)

FAST BALL

    (for WW, Hot for Honorary Installation at Cooperstown)

not just folklore, or
        a tall can of corn (or *Grass* on Cranberry Street)—

to point at the wall and win
        the whole ball of wax . . .

yet
    Walt Whitman

struck out, singing: 'rambled
        all around,
            in & out the town, ram-
      bled til the butchers
            cut him down'

hard from the heels, swung,
        took a notion, had a hankering,
            had good wood, but
            came out—

                a ripple
            in the breeze

bingo! —

        old solitary Whiff-Beard

COBWEBBERY

"The spirit and the will survived, but something in the soul perished."—D. H. LAWRENCE

the best spiders for soup
are the ones under
stones—

ask the man who is one:
plain white american

(not blue gentian red indian yellow sun black carribean)

hard heart, cold
mind's found

a home
in the ground

"a rolling stone, *nolens volens*,
ladles no soup"

maw, rip them boards off
the side the house

and put the soup pot on

and plant us some petunias
in the carcass of the Chevrolet

and let's stay here
and rot in the fields

sit still

THE FLOWER-HUNTER IN THE FIELDS
(for Agnes Arber)

a flame azalea, mayapple, maple, thornapple
plantation

a white cloud in the eye
of a white horse

a field of bluets moving
below the black suit
of William Bartram

bluets; or "Quaker Ladies," or some say
"Innocence"

bluets and the blue of gentians and
Philadelphia blue laws . . .

high hills,

stone cold
sober

as October

H. A. SIEBER

IN 1940, when he was only nine years old, H. A. (Hal) Sieber had his first poem printed in a weekly journal at Brevard, where his father was associated with a paper-manufacturing company. The poem was a prayer for peace in Europe. In high school at Hendersonville, from which he graduated, he wrote "Sonnets to an Atheist." Years later, these two themes still pervaded his mature work.

Herman Alexander Sieber was born at Weehawken, New Jersey, April 5, 1931. After a boyhood in the mountains, he entered the University of North Carolina in 1947. There he studied geology, political science, and law. His undergraduate days were interrupted in 1951 by a government job in Washington, where he met and married Margaret Maureen. Then came several years of military service; and at Fort Benning, Georgia, he organized and led two workshops for writers. He returned to Chapel Hill to complete his degree and manage a supper club. In 1956 he went back to Washington and, while connected with the Senior Specialist Division of the Library of Congress, spent thirteen months of this assignment in an investigation of the case of Ezra Pound on the basis of a Congressional request. His report on the case, which resulted in the release of Pound from St. Elizabeth Hospital, has been published in part. In 1959 Sieber once more returned to Chapel Hill and soon became public relations director for a statewide voluntary health organization. He is the father of two children, a boy and a girl.

Though he admits having felt the influence of Pound and T. S. Eliot, Sieber has charted his own course. A German heritage from his father, and a Catholic upbringing, are obvious throughout the poems. His message is one of hope: though he is aware of the destructive forces in the world, he is assured that man, through religion and poetry, must not be defeated. Sieber is a "wordsmith" (his own term). Often he forges new, unfamiliar words out of old ones, not to obscure his meaning, but to lead the reader into a deeper sense. *In This the Marian Year* (1954) had two reprintings in eight months. *Something the West Will Remember* (1956) confirmed the impression made by the first book.

OAKDALE ANGEL

"... on Gant's porch ... frozen in hard marble silence."
  THOMAS WOLFE in *Look Homeward, Angel*

Sculptured souvenir of the rose wreath wake!
  Do you approve of the cult we make
    Of the graveside tear
      For the unsouled dead?

O marbled emissary from the rumored sphere!
  Why do you throw such longing looks
    At Mrs. Johnson's grassy bed?

OCTOBER

The
Lemming
Leaves wear
Creusa's robe and
Wither on the heaven trees
And one by one the lemming leaves
Are lured or pushed or do they freely fall
(Fall is the Leitmotif) and slumber
On the bottomland unknowing do
They know the bottoms are
The outstretched
Palm of
God.

Nomen ineffabile is winter full moon
And the lemming leaves fall to the bottomland
(Full is the Leitmotif) and in October
Gown the bottoms' climbing lemmings

And climbing lemmings
  Falling lemming leaves
    Together sleep.

                    Und unbekannt
                    Bleibt Göttes Hand.

ON THE MAKE-UP OF A POET

A poem
is a conversation
between poets, whether the poets
are man and man
or God and man.

How dare you say
that Sandburg doesn't see
God when he looks at the
goats
at Connemara?

How dare you say . . .

Or that Joe Smith, poet,
didn't see God
on the Hill of Cumorah
or somewhere?

Or Ezra Pound, the nut
who writes the cantos,
do you dare to say
that God didn't mumble when
He talked to him
and he wrote it down?

What right have you to say
that Tom Wolfe of Asheville
and Brooklyn, New York,
didn't talk all the time
all the time with God
in Asheville
and
Brooklyn, New York?

BLUE RIDGE PARKWAY

"... a beautiful drive through Western Virginia and North Carolina ..."
AAA Brochure

Before the sun was scuttled
I saw the "southern part
of heaven" all day long.
The world about the parkway
sparkled like a gold piece
... before the sun was scuttled.

The cottony fog and blue haze
were soaked up by the hills
before dusk turned to night,
and now at quarter past
the big black hills balloon
and squirm and rise
like dragonbulls
from the greenblack fury.

Run! Run!
The sun is scuttled.

THE SAINT AND THE POET

The saint and the poet
from their brown mound sourleaved American graves
talked without proof about the autopsies in question
and decided that the quotidian reminders
of our zooid heritage
called for, could use a new code
from this old litany:

am chrismon
am monkey's brother
is another
am neither
am both of these rather
a wordsmith by trade.

SOMETHING THE WEST WILL REMEMBER

Something the west will remember
is hope. Will remember
when the poets began dying when
the world: (Third) was succeeded by the
fourth when the bawbeeworth heavenism
overconverted this gipsyry of then.
Something the west will remember
is hope.

AN H-BOMB EVENING DOWN

An H-bomb evening down of man
unchartering our civility
would leave no argument nor landscape
nor legislature nor ark or survival
from which to begin again.
I see in evenings such as this
a certain finality,
a definite toolateness for hope
or tolerance or corrective upheaval,
moreover, the death still inability
to retrieve the Judas kiss.

Such an H-bomb evening down
trembling in pigeon milk and blood clot
would echo with a sacrosanct profanity
from the genital millpool, scream
for a noah shadkhan,
"Shadkhan Shadkhan! bring your umbrella."
I would not count on even a goat
to live through this inning of finity.
I see in this evening down the same
sort of death that hungers in wait
on the outer rim of hell's belly.

FROM THE ALEMBIC

From the alembic of my alchemy: sun,
moon, and wind: boil out this poet's stone:
love conjoined with hope. Build me a world
on love and hope, and I will show you
the courage of the sun and moon's defense
and I will show you the way that the moon remembers
when the wars are over and the law fulfilled.

So fragrant the blood of this transubstantiation.
So fragrant the blood that boils on the sun.
So fragrant, ai, that cools in the moon.
So fragrant the blood that draws this way
in the wind's defiance of the death of us,
in the wind's compliance with the sign
of the cross.

A POSTURE FOR NEXT YEAR

Even infinity has epochs and hierarchies of days
        lets yesterdays grow dimmer
        gives each today its own
        tomorrow and each tomorrow
        a vanishing successor.

Nächstes Jahr Wird's besser,
        he confided as he slumped
        into a posture for next year.
        All of a sudden, it was time
        for hearing reassembled echoes of a former voice:
Immer nächstes Jahr.

THAT'S ALL SHE WROTE

"I love you"
    That's the word she used:
    "love"—and then
    she died (the word I need
    is "vanished") then she
    vanished, then, and then
    I redeyed read the words
      "I love you" and to my younger self
That's all she wrote.

She vanished and
That's all she wrote.
      "Love" "Love" "Love"
      The word defines itself so slowly
      Even parsed on paper
      Scented and flowered with "I love
      you" for rereading.
"Love" is a girl's
Four-letter word with moving parts.

INDEX TO POEMS

Actor, The
   James Sexton Layton   50
Apology
   Paul Bartlett   23
As You Are, My Friend
   Vernon Ward   53
Au Beau Milieu
   Frank Borden Hanes   88
Aunt Ella
   Guy Owen   109

Baby-Sitter Blues
   Edith Earnshaw   27
Be
   Will Inman   105
Birth
   Olive Tilford Dargan   10
Birthplace
   James Larkin Pearson   7
Blotting Paper
   Thad Stem, Jr.   71
Blown Newspaper, A
   Will Inman   104
Blue Ridge Parkway
   H. A. Sieber   134
Bowl of October, A
   Helen Bevington   45
Boy on the Back of a Wagon
   Thad Stem, Jr.   76
Buck Duke and Mamma
   Eleanor Ross Taylor   94

Cardinal
   Zoe Kincaid Brockman   36
Carol
   Charles Edward Eaton   80
Carolina Wrens
   Edith Earnshaw   28
Christmas Eve
   Zoe Kincaid Brockman   39
Church Bell—Winter Time
   Thad Stem, Jr.   71
City Rain
   Paul Bartlett   24
Cobwebbery
   Jonathan Williams   129

Cold Wind Blows, A
   Zoe Kincaid Brockman   37
Compleat Swimmer, The
   Charles Edward Eaton   80
Concerning Wings
   Zoe Kincaid Brockman   36
Conspiracy, The
   Guy Owen   110
Copperhead
   Charles Edward Eaton   82
Country Saga, A
   Sam Ragan   67
Courthouse Bell
   Thad Stem, Jr.   73
Credo
   Jonathan Williams   127
Crepe Myrtle
   Charles Edward Eaton   82
Crime and Punishment
   James Sexton Layton   49
Crisis
   Thad Stem, Jr.   72

Deep Summer, after Midnight
   Thad Stem, Jr.   76
Deer Hunt
   Sam Ragan   67
Deserted Farm
   Guy Owen   111
Deserted House
   Sam Ragan   68
Dilation
   Will Inman   102
Distance in Your Touch, The
   Will Inman   104
Dream Is Not Enough, The
   Zoe Kincaid Brockman   38

Erosion
   James Larkin Pearson   6

Fads and Fancies
   Edith Earnshaw   30
Far Bugles
   Olive Tilford Dargan   10
Fast Ball
   Jonathan Williams   128

Fifty Acres	
James Larkin Pearson	2
Finale	
Paul Bartlett	23
Find Out Moonshine	
Helen Bevington	47
First Man on Venus	
Robert Watson	113
Flower-Hunter in the Fields, The	
Jonathan Williams	130
From the Alembic	
H. A. Sieber	136
Girl in a Library, A	
Randall Jarrell	60
Girl with Guitar	
O. B. Hardison, Jr.	119
God	
James Larkin Pearson	3
Granddaughter	
Eleanor Ross Taylor	98
Gray Horizons	
Sam Ragan	65
Guest Room	
Olive Tilford Dargan	16
Halloween: A Poem for Children	
Robert Watson	113
Hawk	
Guy Owen	109
H-Bomb Evening Down, An	
H. A. Sieber	135
He Gave Up Golf	
Edith Earnshaw	33
He Will Make the Grade	
Edith Earnshaw	27
Heart Path	
Vernon Ward	58
Here Is Wisdom	
James Larkin Pearson	4
Hidden Scars	
Sam Ragan	65
Homer in a Garden	
James Larkin Pearson	3

Homeward Song	
Olive Tilford Dargan	16
Hunger and Rain	
Sam Ragan	69
I Ain't No Candidate	
James Larkin Pearson	5
I Felt Like Slapping Him	
Edith Earnshaw	31
I Say to the Mountain	
Zoe Kincaid Brockman	37
Impressions	
O. B. Hardison, Jr.	120
In an Editor's Office	
Zoe Kincaid Brockman	36
In Labyrinths	
Frank Borden Hanes	87
In the Churchyard	
Eleanor Ross Taylor	95
In the Headlights	
Charles Edward Eaton	84
It Is Not the Sea	
Guy Owen	107
Just a Breeze	
Edith Earnshaw	32
Lèse Majesté	
Paul Bartlett	24
Line of Life, The	
James Sexton Layton	51
Little Saucers, Big Saucers	
Thad Stem, Jr.	78
Love Is a Bullet	
Frank Borden Hanes	90
Love-Death Story, A	
Charles Edward Eaton	83
Love's Ending	
Paul Bartlett	25
Lyric	
Will Inman	101
Madame	
Eleanor Ross Taylor	96
Magnolia Belt, The	
Helen Bevington	46

INDEX TO POEMS 141

Man Raking Leaves
  Thad Stem, Jr. 75
Middle Passage
  O. B. Hardison, Jr. 122
Miss Flo
  Edith Earnshaw 28
Miss Sallie's Chowchow
  Edith Earnshaw 29
Mixed Emotions
  Vernon Ward 55
Morning Window
  Olive Tilford Dargan 17
Most Wanted
  Robert Watson 113
My Old Man
  Edith Earnshaw 31

New Letter Writer, The
  Helen Bevington 47
Night in June, A
  James Larkin Pearson 4
Notes for an Autobiography
  Charles Edward Eaton 85

Oakdale Angel
  H. A. Sieber 132
October
  H. A. Sieber 132
October Days
  James Larkin Pearson 7
Of Dust and Stars
  Vernon Ward 54
Of Motion
  O. B. Hardison, Jr. 118
Of Violets
  Vernon Ward 56
Old Arrowhead Thoughts of
  a Late War
  Frank Borden Hanes 88
Old Chimney
  Edith Earnshaw 34
Old Hunter
  Guy Owen 108
Old Hup
  Thad Stem, Jr. 72

Old Man's Fancy
  Thad Stem, Jr. 73
Old Tobey
  Guy Owen 110
On Seven Hills
  Will Inman 103
On Stage, Off Stage
  Robert Watson 116
On the Make-Up of a Poet
  H. A. Sieber 133
One-Talent Man
  James Larkin Pearson 8
Ouch!
  Edith Earnshaw 29
Our Dusk: That West
  Jonathan Williams 127

Paging Professor Gooseberry
  Thad Stem, Jr. 75
Plain Man, The
  Frank Borden Hanes 87
Poetry Revival
  Frank Borden Hanes 89
Portrait
  Sam Ragan 68
Post Card
  Thad Stem, Jr. 77
Posture for Next Year, A
  H. A. Sieber 136
Primitivism
  O. B. Hardison, Jr. 118
"Prophet, The"
  Sam Ragan 66
Puppy
  Edith Earnshaw 29

Query
  Edith Earnshaw 34

Report from the Carolinas
  Helen Bevington 42
Roommates
  James Larkin Pearson 3
Rough Day, The
  Jonathan Williams 125

Saint and the Poet, The
   H. A. Sieber — 134
School Days
   Thad Stem, Jr. — 74
September Winds
   Helen Bevington — 46
Sick Child, A
   Randall Jarrell — 60
So Independently the Cedars Grow
   Paul Bartlett — 25
Solitary Horseman, The
   Guy Owen — 108
Something More
   Thad Stem, Jr. — 74
Something the West Will Remember
   H. A. Sieber — 135
Song
   Eleanor Ross Taylor — 93
Sorrow's Day
   Zoe Kincaid Brockman — 39
Speculations
   O. B. Hardison, Jr. — 122
Spin, A
   Jonathan Williams — 126
Split-Rail Fence
   Guy Owen — 111
St. Petersburg Paradox, The
   O. B. Hardison, Jr. — 119
Street in North Carolina, A
   Helen Bevington — 45
Summer Excursion: Signs and Portents
   Helen Bevington — 44
Sure Signs
   Thad Stem, Jr. — 71

That's All She Wrote
   H. A. Sieber — 137

They Roasted Me Instead
   Edith Earnshaw — 27
Three Cinquains
   Zoe Kincaid Brockman — 40
3 Sit-Ins Agin
   Jonathan Williams — 124
To Ford, Guggenheim, Rockefeller, Etc.
   O. B. Hardison, Jr. — 121
To the Lost Colony
   Zoe Kincaid Brockman — 40
Tree Will Mow Thickets
   Will Inman — 102
Two Cats Make the World
   Vernon Ward — 55
Two Little Houses
   Edith Earnshaw — 28
Two Teacups
   Vernon Ward — 57

Uncle
   Eleanor Ross Taylor — 97

Waves, The
   Charles Edward Eaton — 81
Way of Looking, A
   Helen Bevington — 46
What in the World!
   Edith Earnshaw — 32
Where Willow Is a Limber Switch
   Will Inman — 101
White Stallion, The
   Guy Owen — 107
Wild Garden
   James Larkin Pearson — 6
Winter Lovers
   Robert Watson — 114

Your Footsteps on the Stair
   Zoe Kincaid Brockman — 38

www.ingramcontent.com/pod-product-compliance
Lightning Source LLC
Chambersburg PA
CBHW030114010526
44116CB00005B/245